A Country Camera
1844-1914

By the same author:

The Horseman's Weekend Book
Ourselves in Canada (jointly with Elspeth)
Past Positive

A Country Camera
1844-1914

*Rural life as depicted in photographs
from the early days of photography to the
outbreak of the First World War*

GORDON WINTER

DAVID & CHARLES: NEWTON ABBOT

*Distributed in the United States by the Gale Research Company,
Book Tower, Detroit, 48226*

For
S

0 7153 5245 8

First published in 1966 by Country Life Limited
This edition first published in 1971 by
David & Charles (Publishers) Limited
South Devon House Newton Abbot Devon
Reprinted 1972

Printed in Great Britain by Redwood Press Ltd Trowbridge Wiltshire

Contents

Illustrations

Acknowledgments

I am indebted to the following for permission to make quotations in the text: from Thomas Hardy's novels and poems, Macmillan and Co. Ltd, and the trustees of the Hardy estate; from Flora Thompson's trilogy, *Lark Rise to Candleford*, the Oxford University Press; and from George Sturt's *A Small Boy in the 60's*, the Cambridge University Press.

I am grateful to the following for lending me the photographs in this book, and for their kindness and courtesy in helping me with my research. Plates 1, 45, 59, 95, 107, the Science Museum, South Kensington. 2, 4, 48, 49, 86, 89, 96, 116, 156, the Curtis Museum, Alton, Hants. 3, 5, 27, 31, 47, 58, 91, 92, 93, 102, 103, 104, 110, 134, 135, 154, Northumberland Record Office, Newcastle-upon-Tyne. 6, 18, 29, 60, 63, 120, 125, 127, 131, 140, 146, 151, 155, W. E. R. Hall-garth, Scartho, Lincs. 7, 8, 11, 12, 13, 14, 16, 22, 24, 57, 81, 124, 130, Warwickshire Photographic Survey, Birmingham Public Reference Library. 9, 43, R. A. Salaman and G. J. Moody. 10, 21, 41, 46, 65, 69, 71, 106, Hereford City Library. 15, Miss A. C. Hastie. 17, 20, 23, 39, 56, 66, 67, 68, 70, 72, 90, 98, 105, 129, the Museum of English Rural Life, University of Reading. 19, 62, 114, 147, Merioneth County Record Office. 25, Christopher Hussey. 26, 28, Professor J. H. Hutton. 30, 40, 44, 82, 87, 115, 123, 128, 149, 150, 152, 153, Suffolk Photographic Survey. 32, Miss F. R. Gaman. 33, Miss Cicely Smelt. 34, T. A. Mc-Dowell. 35, J. Gordon Davies. 36, 37, 85, 108, 145, Borough of Hove Central Library. 38, 52, 53, 80, 97, 113, 132, 139, Wiltshire Archaeological and Natural History Society. 42, 50, 54, Norwich Central Library. 51, Welsh Folk Museum, St Fagans, Cardiff. 55, Mrs M. Robb. 61, 73, 74, 76, 122, 138, County Record Office, Huntingdon. 64, Rennie Bere. 75, from *The Old Hand-Knitters of the Dales*, by Marie Hartley and Joan Ingilby (Dalesman Pub-lishing Co.). 77, 144, Gloucestershire County Records Office. 78, Mrs Wilson Jameson. 79, 84, 99, Miss M. Wight. 83, F. C. Morgan. 88, Gordon Smith. 94, 121, 141, 142, Newcastle-upon-Tyne, City Libraries. 100, Bedford County Record Office. 101, 109, 117, 133, 148, Essex County Record Office. 111, 126, Salop County Record Office. 112, 136, Buckingham County Record Office. 118, 119, 137, Surrey County Library, Farnham, by courtesy of Lady Knight. 143, British Rail, London Midland Region. 157, John L. Gilbert. 158, Taskers of Andover, Ltd.

Introduction

If those who turn through these pages obtain from them a small part of the pleasure and satisfaction that I enjoyed in searching for the photographs, and in putting the book together, I shall be well content. When I first started work on this book I was under the deluded impression that early photographs of English country life would be easy to come by; that all I needed to do was to ask the Editor of *Country Life* to print a suitable letter from me, and that scores of admirable photographs would come pouring through the post into my lap. This was not quite how things turned out. A few kind persons did send me photographs in answer to my published appeal, and of those few, a few were of sufficient photographic quality for reproduction, and have found their way into these pages. But in the end it was clear that if I wanted to find the photographs that I knew must exist, I should have to go out and look for them. In that pursuit I visited the offices of county archivists and county librarians, and called on the curators of local museums, over much of England and Wales, from Northumberland and Merioneth to Gloucestershire and Hampshire. Everywhere I met with the greatest kindness, and with a keen recognition of the value of early photographs as documents in social history. Problems of time and distance prevented my visiting collections in Scotland, and therefore this survey regretfully stops at the Border.

Some of the photographs that I was able to bring back were discovered in unexpected circumstances. The two pictures of the smithy on page 57, for example, were originally part of a large collection of glass negatives that were left in the cottage of a nineteenth-century photographer after his death. The new occupant of the cottage was not greatly interested in the documentary or pictorial value of this store of negatives, but felt nevertheless that they ought to be put to some good use. Being a practical man he therefore employed them to build cloches for his lettuces: one row of plates thrust into the earth along each side, and another row neatly placed over the top. Under the circumstances it is not surprising that only a few of the negatives were still capable of producing photographic prints when they were finally rescued.

The rescue of photographs from a lettuce-bed, however, fades into insignificance when it is compared with what might have happened to the negatives at Lacock Abbey in Wiltshire, from which the earliest prints in my selection are taken. It was at Lacock Abbey that the negative-positive process of photography was invented by that remarkable country gentleman, William Henry Fox Talbot. He made his first photographs, in 1834 and 1835, with a camera developed by him from a *camera obscura*. His negatives, on flimsy sheets of writing paper, were made by what he called the calotype process, the first photographic method to utilise the chemical development of the latent image produced by briefly exposing silver salts to light. In 1937 these first negatives, and thousands of the very earliest photographs taken between 1835 and 1847, still lay in a cupboard at Lacock Abbey where they had remained virtually unseen for 90 years. It can only be regarded as something of a miracle that during all that time some well-intentioned tidier-up did not seize upon this priceless store as unwanted clutter, and burn the lot. Happily they were preserved, and were presented to the Science Museum, South

Kensington, by Fox Talbot's grand-daughter, Miss Matilda Talbot. There they are now treasured, and I am indebted to Dr D. B. Thomas for showing me the Lacock photographs (Plates 1, 59 and 107). A full account of the discovery and early use of the negative-positive process will be found in Dr Thomas's own monograph, *The First Negatives*.

When I started collecting these photographs I did not set out with the intention of presenting any kind of ordered survey of social life in rural England before 1914, but merely of providing some glimpses of what country life used to be like, as recorded by the camera. Nevertheless, the photographs that I have been fortunate enough to find do tell us something of England's social history, in a way that is often more vivid than the written word. No kind of profit-and-loss account can be drawn up from these pages because the evidence is too casual and haphazard; whether these countrymen and countrywomen appear healthier, happier or wiser than their successors is debatable and perhaps irrelevant. What is certain is that they were different, or at least that they led very different lives. They enjoyed an ordered and comparatively peaceful existence against a background that had changed little for many hundreds of years. Each one of them occupied a clearly defined place in the social order and knew exactly where he stood. He could, of course, move about within the social order; English history is full of the sound of clogs moving upstairs and of satin skirts coming down. But the background of social life in the countryside must have seemed as fixed and permanent as the hills. It remained so until August, 1914. From that month everything changed. The photograph on the last page, showing men from the Wiltshire countryside leaving Calne to join up, records the precise moment when the English countryside had reached the end of an era.

Although photography did not begin until the 1830s, some of these pictures take us back considerably further into historical time. One of the splendid old men in the group in Plate 20 is known to have fought, as a drummer-boy, at Waterloo. And the fine portrait of Robert Morvinson (Plate 63), the carrier and shoemaker of Stallingborough in Lincolnshire, was taken in 1857. The old man was 82 when this photograph was taken; that is to say, he was born in 1775. So here is a photograph of a man who was born when the United States was still a British Colony.

Anyone whose appetite is whetted by the 159 photographs here presented should visit the Museum of English Rural Life at the University of Reading, where there is a very large collection of such photographs and where an admirable historic record is to be found in the files. I am greatly indebted to Mr Andrew Jewell, the Keeper of the museum, and to Miss Margaret Fuller, Assistant Keeper, for providing me with a number of my photographs and for helping me with some of the technical information in the captions. I am also particularly grateful to Miss Sally Sanderson for her help in research in county archives and similar sources; to Mr John Nevinson for helping me to date some of the pictures by the clothing worn; to Mr and Mrs R. G. Pratt for their warm hospitality and for the excellent pictures from the Suffolk Photographic Survey; to the many county archivists and county librarians who devoted so much time, often at week-ends, to helping me in my search through their photograph files; and to the individuals who sent me treasured pictures, often from family albums, not all of whom have the satisfaction of seeing their photographs printed here.

1   A couple at table at Lacock Abbey, Wiltshire, in 1844. This is not only one of the earliest photographs in the book; it is one of the earliest of its kind in existence. A brief account of the development of the negative-positive process of photography at Lacock Abbey by William Henry Fox Talbot will be found in the Introduction, on page 9. The characters in the picture are not known, but are probably members of the Fox Talbot family. They might well, by their appearance, be Robert Browning and Elizabeth Barrett; in fact, the celebrated elopement took place in 1846, two years after the photograph was taken.

Domestic life

Since the quality of domestic life depends entirely on the characters of those who take part in it, and scarcely at all on their external circumstances, it is pointless to ask whether the families in the photographs that follow look happier than their great grandchildren or grandchildren. The Victorians and Edwardians are unlikely to have been any happier or unhappier in their home lives than the primitive British who lived in holes in the ground at Maiden Castle. What these photographs illustrate is not the quality of life, but its trappings, and these have changed vastly. In upper middle-class homes large numbers of servants meant more leisure for the family who employed them and also, I suspect, more leisure for the servants themselves. Where there were no servants, quite a large proportion of each day in the home must have been spent on such simple tasks as lighting fires and drawing water, tasks on which we spend no more time than it takes to turn a tap or press a switch.

2 'Our domestics — 1865.' This is a companion picture to the photograph of the Curtis family playing croquet, taken the same year, Plate 96. The description 'our domestics' is written on the mounted photograph in ink, with the date — clearly by a member of the Curtis family. This confirms that all six women are in fact members of the domestic staff. Their status is not at all apparent from the photograph, which suggests how far we may sometimes be wrong in our conception of the rigid barriers that divided the layers of Victorian society. Gardeners of today may be surprised to see such an advanced lawn-mower just over one hundred years ago. It must have been heavy to use. The stalwart gardener with the side-whiskers needed the help of the gardener's boy to propel it; the boy walked in front of the grass-box, pulling the handle on which he has placed his right hand in this picture. The handle swung forward in use.

3 Gathering wood for the domestic hearth: a photograph by David Dippie Dixon, the historian of Coquetdale. This shows the opposite end of the social scale from that in the two preceding photographs, though the young woman looks sturdy enough. The rough road on which she is standing may well have been chosen by the photographer to provide his subject with a symbolic setting.

12

4 A woman sitting by her stove in the Rothbury district of Northumberland in about 1890. This is probably the kind of stove for which the wood in Plate 3 was destined. The photograph has succeeded in capturing something of the tough, rather grim quality of North Country life.

5 Interior of a cottage in Northumberland, around the turn of the century. This is possibly a more luxurious hearth than that for which the North Country girl in Plate 3 is gathering fuel. What makes the picture particularly interesting is the dog-spit, the curious drum-like object above the cupboard on the left of the fireplace. In the eighteenth century dog-spits were common, though this one would have been a rare antiquity when the photograph was taken. Small dogs were placed inside the wheel, and were trained to walk in it, causing it to turn like a treadmill. The power was used to turn a roasting spit at the fire.

6 Harry Calvert at the killing of the family pig, Lincolnshire, 1905. I had some hesitation in including this photograph in case it should offend the susceptibilities of readers accustomed to seeing their meat only under the detached conditions of the supermarket. But I have put it in because the killing of the family pig was such an important event in the life of almost every English cottage family at the time. Flora Thompson, in *Lark Rise*, describes how the family lived at close quarters with their pig until he was of a size to kill, cherishing him and feeding him with all the scraps that were available.

'The family pig was everybody's pride and everybody's business. Mother spent hours boiling up the "little taturs" to mash and mix with the pot-liquor, in which food had been cooked, to feed the pig for its evening meal and help out the expensive barley meal. The children, on their way home from school, would fill their arms with sow thistle, dandelion, and choice long grass, or roam along the hedgerows on wet evenings collecting snails in a pail for the pig's supper.' The authoress also describes the rather horrific killing, but remarks: 'Country people of the day had little sympathy for the sufferings of animals, and men, women, and children would gather round to see the sight.'

7 The cottage pump at Wellesbourne Hastings, Warwickshire, 1895. The farmhouse kitchen in the next photograph almost certainly did not have water on tap; water would have been fetched from a pump like the one shown here — though this is a comparatively 'modern' pump of cast iron. The pump itself, which we today would regard as a laborious way of getting water, was regarded as a much-to-be-desired labour-saving device by housewives who had only a well, or possibly only a neighbour's well. Drawing a bucket of water from the pump was a great deal quicker and easier than lowering a bucket into a well and hauling it up again. I spent part of my own early childhood in a farmhouse where a well was the only source of drinking water, though water for washing could be obtained more easily by putting a dipper into the rainwater butt.

8   The kitchen at Ram Hall, Berkswell, Warwickshire, in July, 1892. This is an interesting picture of a country kitchen of the last century, because it was obviously taken without anybody first tidying the place up; it shows it as it really was, in normal use. Notice that the kettle hangs over the fire — it does not stand on it. The fire itself needs the use of bellows (far left), from time to time. There is evidently no separate laundry in this house, or the mangle (right) would not have been in the kitchen. The lunch basket has been put out either for a working-day's lunch in the fields, or possibly for a fishing picnic.

9   A shepherd of the Berkshire Downs in 1890. This photograph of a shepherd and his wife at their cottage door shows many signs of having been posed by the photographer in an attempt to imitate a Dutch painting of the seventeenth century, prints of which were being widely sold when this photograph was taken. The wash basin and jugs on the table to the left may always have been kept there, but I suspect that they were carefully put out for the sake of the photograph. The same 'Dutch' influence is even more noticeable in the next picture.

10 The cottage door, Herefordshire, about 1900. Here is another photograph plainly taken with the influence of Vermeer or Pieter de Hooch in mind. The 'props', though, are genuine enough. Present-day susceptibilities are outraged by the small-ness of the jay's cage on the right. The cage on the left also appears to be occupied, but I cannot make out whether the occupant is a rabbit or a bird.

11   A cottage at Tiddington, Warwickshire, in 1889. An interesting point about this picture is how little the tenor of rural life had changed between the date when the house was built and the date when the photograph was taken; whereas in the past seven decades it has altered beyond all recognition.

12 Gossiping at the cottage door, Barston, Warwickshire, 1890. The little girl's mother has not thought it necessary to protect the child's head with a hat (compare this with Plate 14), possibly because the sun was not strong enough.

13 Village children at Hill Wootton, Warwickshire, in August, 1890. The immediate question —
which of them are boys and which are girls — has an easy answer. The ones with short hair, who
look like boys, are boys. They are wearing skirts and pinafores because custom and household
economy demanded that the boys should wear their older sister's clothes as they grew into them.
This did not produce the taunting, and subsequent bloody noses, that one might suppose. Other
little boys in the village suffered the same indignity, but without in fact feeling that it was any great
affront to their manhood. The age when you graduated into trousers depended on whether, and
when, the family possessed a pair that would fit you.

Children

Looking at the faces of the children in these pictures, it is tempting to compare them with their
successors today and to ask which look the happier and the healthier. Personally, I doubt
whether any conclusion can be reached. The children of poorer families in the villages of
sixty or one hundred years ago ate less varied food, and not infrequently were hungry; but the
food that they did eat was probably better of its kind. Flora Thompson, in *Lark Rise to
Candleford*, paints a vivid picture of village children on their way to school, happily supplementing their slender breakfast with what the fields and hedgerows provided. Education in the
three R's was already universal, or nearly so; but many countrymen regarded it as no more
than a mixed blessing. There was so much that the countryman had to learn which he could
never find in books. And old Captain Vye, in Hardy's *The Return of the Native*, must have
expressed the opinion of many of his contemporaries when he declared: 'There's too much of
that sending to school in these days! It only does harm. Every gatepost and barn's door you
come to is sure to have some bad word or other chalked upon it by the young rascals: a
woman can hardly pass for shame sometimes.'

14 The back door of a cottage at Upper Tysoe: April, 1895. The baby is evidently wearing the latest thing in Easter bonnets. The tendency to put very small children in very large hats is noticeable in several photographs of the period. I can only suppose that it was connected with the belief that too much sun was bad for you.

21

15   A goat cart at Duffield, Derbyshire, in 1906. Miss A. C. Hastie, who sent me this charming photograph, writes: 'The goat carriage was a great pleasure to children, and the goat could be driven like a pony. I trained it to harness myself. The people in the photograph are myself, at the goat's head, and my two sisters. The goat lived to the good age of fifteen years.'

16   The doorway of Arden Cottage, Aston Cantlow, Warwickshire, in the 1890's. This little boy, obviously rather pleased with himself, may be out at the knees of his breeches, but he has escaped the girlish fate of his contemporaries in the first picture in this section.

17 A donkey trap in a Herefordshire village in 1910. This was a good deal better than today's school bus. One is inclined to forget the role played by donkeys in rural transport, perhaps because the horse has survived, whereas the donkey is a rarity. The prevalence of donkeys a hundred years ago makes it easier to understand Betsey Trotwood, David Copperfield's aunt, who could bear any affront except the sight of donkeys on the green in front of her cottage.

18 The village school treat at Waltham, Lincolnshire, in the first week of August, 1914. The secure world in which these children and their parents had lived was about to crumble for ever. The grown-ups in this picture must already have been aware of the cloud that was hanging over them; though no-one forsaw the magnitude of the cloud — and anyway, it was not going to be allowed to spoil the children's treat.

Old age

As almost every serious nineteenth-century novelist has made plain, the underlying fear among countryfolk who were not well off was that, when old age overtook them, they might be forced to leave their cottages and be driven to live in the workhouse. This was felt to be not merely distressing and uncomfortable in itself, though it frequently involved the separation of married couples; it was felt to be a terrible disgrace. Though in many ways our lives have not changed for the better since the photographs in this book were taken, the security that our modern conception of the Welfare State has brought to old people is a gain that can hardly be overestimated.

19   Roland and Betsy Jones of Hen Hafod, Merioneth, in 1870. The highly respectable couple in this photograph were less fortunate than Rough Jimmy in Plate 23, though they were luckier than many of their contemporaries. We know nothing of the details of their circumstances, though it is clear from their bearing, and their tidy and well-kept clothes, that they were in no way a feckless or improvident couple. All we know of them is the inscription in Welsh on the back of the photograph, which reads: 'They entered the workhouse at Bala, but instead of separating them the Guardians permitted them to have a room to themselves.'

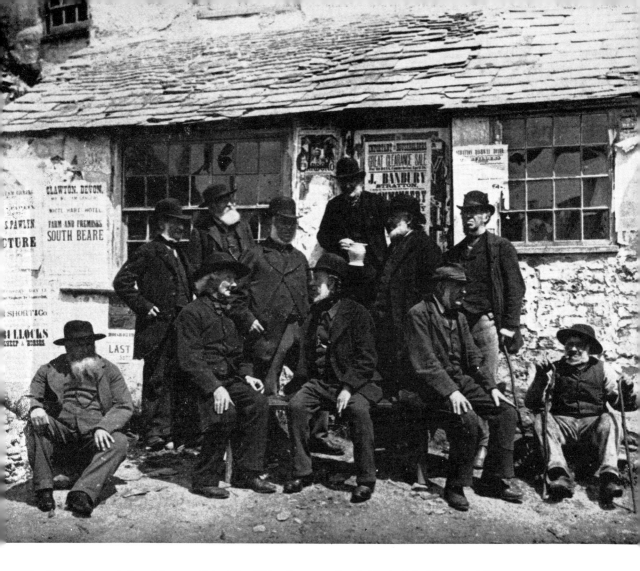

20 Stout-hearted Cornishmen of the 80s. This photograph of elderly inhabitants of Stratton, near Bude in Cornwall, in 1887, shows them in their best suits and must have been taken on an important occasion, though we do not know what it was. Fortunately, however, we do know the occupation of each of the men shown. The dapper little man on the left in the back row was a clerk, and was agent for the Grenville property, and as such no doubt enjoyed a somewhat superior social position. Next to him, from left to right, are the watchmaker, the cordwainer, the carpenter (holding the jug), the shoemaker and the ironworker; he was also the owner of a bobbery pack of hounds (which may account for his somewhat lordly air). Seated, from left to right, are the blacksmith, the barber (who was also precentor of the Wesleyan chapel and has a somewhat other-worldly expression), the auctioneer, who was also a printer, another shoemaker and, on the right on the ground, a labourer. The remarkable thing about this labourer is that he had been a drummer-boy at Waterloo. He must have been in his late eighties when the photograph was taken, and would no doubt have been about fifteen as a drummer-boy. This must be one of the very few photographs of a man who actually fought at Waterloo.

An interesting point about the picture is that the occupations given above were not, so far as I know, former occupations, but those being carried out by these old men at the time when the photograph was taken. Continuing to work after what we automatically think of as 'retiring age' was obviously a necessity for most country people in the days before the Old Age Pension.

21 A Herefordshire dame of about 1890. Though the general atmosphere of the photograph suggests a warm day, the old lady was taking no chances with the weather and has a rug over her arm in addition to her shawl — the latter possibly an example of the fashion for plaid shawls set by Queen Victoria. The cotton umbrella, and particularly the fastening round it, could have belonged to Sarah Gamp herself, and would have been used in summer to protect the old lady as much from the sun as from the rain. The frilled cap that she is wearing under her bonnet was a long-outmoded fashion in the 1890s, when the photograph was probably taken; it was known as a morning cap, and was fashionable in the 1850s and 60s.

22 An old villager of Ashow in Warwickshire, in 1903. The newspaper that he is reading makes no concession to popular appeal — it carries columns of solid type unbroken by headlines — though this was the time of the beginning of the popular press. The news seems undisturbing; the Boer War was just over, Edward VII safely on the throne, the Unionists in power with a comfortable majority; but Joe Chamberlain was already threatening the peace of the Cabinet by his shocking proposal for fair trade rather than free trade — that is to say, tariff preference for British colonies.

23   Rough Jimmy. In 1901, when this photograph was taken, James Minns, or Rough Jimmy as he was called, was claimed to be the oldest woodcutter in England. This was probably true, because he was born in Ditchingham, Norfolk, in the year 1826, so he was seventy-five when the photograph was taken. In fact he had by that time given up his old calling of tree-felling because his eyesight was failing, but he was earning what he could by splitting branches to be used for thatching stacks. The photograph shows him in the act of 'riving', as it was called, and in spite of his failing sight he is recorded as having been able to do the work quickly and skilfully. He did not earn enough to live on, however, and the authorities decided to send him to the workhouse. In common with all independent-minded countrymen of his day, he regarded this as the worst fate that could befall him, and said: 'I'd sooner lie down and die by the side of the road, and I'd do it too.' When this news reached the big house, the squire announced that he would allow Rough Jimmy a free cottage and a shilling a week for the rest of his life, and it was hoped that with what he could still earn he would be able to manage. But it is an example of the attitude to the problems of old age only seventy years ago that a letter about Rough Jimmy's case was published in *Country Life* at the time, with the comment: 'Possibly some charitable person will come forward and offer some assistance to this hardworking woodman, or life will be a sore struggle during the remainder of his few declining years.'

24 Cottagers at Hampton Lucy in Warwickshire, in 1890. The three characters in Plates 22 and 24
were fortunate in their day in that old age did not involve them in being uprooted from their homes.
Both the photographs show signs of rather careful posing — no doubt by the photographer rather
than by his subjects, in the search for a result that looked a little like a painting.

The Squire

25 Throughout the period covered by this book the squire was so much a patriarchal figure that it is appropriate to have a photograph of him surrounded by his family. Edward Hussey (1807–1894) inherited the Scotney Castle estate from his father at the age of ten, and was thus squire for sixty-six years, from the time when he attained his majority in 1828. Contemporary with Gladstone at Christ Church, Oxford, he was a forthright Conservative, but confined his public activities to local administration, as befitted a squire, in the counties of Kent and Sussex, in both of which his estate lay. He was a competent amateur architect and antiquarian and he decided, when he was thirty, that instead of modernising the old moated manor-house of Scotney, he would build a new one on a healthier site that overlooked the little medieval 'castle', which he partly dismantled to form a picturesque ruin. He engaged Salvin to execute his carefully formulated conception in a restrained and practical Elizabethan idiom. The building of the new house and the creation of the romantic landscape that links it with the old (the planting of which he carried out) were the outstanding achievement of himself and his wife, Henrietta Windsor-Clive, whom he married in 1853; they had four sons and two daughters. A venerated figure, perhaps more typically Georgian than Victorian, he lived to see all his plans fulfilled in ripe old age.

The Church

Even today the Church exerts more influence in the villages and the countryside than it does in industrial towns and cities; in the nineteenth century, and in the early years of the twentieth century, its power and prestige in rural England were still unchallenged. The photographs in this section give a revealing glimpse of what the country parson was like and of how he lived.

26   The Reverend Joseph Henry Hutton, Rector of West Heslerton in the East Riding of Yorkshire, with his family and staff, getting in the hay in 1892. The Rector farmed part of his own glebe. That great upholder of the principle that a country parson ought to live comfortably, Archdeacon Grantly, of *Barchester Towers*, might not have approved of the Rector's family actually taking part in the manual labour of haymaking; but there is no doubt that the day-to-day business of farming was as much in the mind of the incumbent of Plumstead Episcopi as it was in that of every country parson of his day. The Rector in the photograph is, of course, the patriarchal, bearded figure in the

centre of the group. Others in the picture are his seven-year-old son Jack, by the top of the ladder, now Professor J. H. Hutton, to whom I am indebted for this photograph; Margaret Hutton, his half-sister, on the ladder; on top of the rick from left to right, Benjamin Bean, the Rector's groom-gardener and general factotum; Alfred Hutton, the Rector's second son, and at that time his curate; young Roger Hutton, aged five; and Fred Horsley, the village bootmaker, who made, as well as mended, all the Hutton family's shoes. The two women standing on the hay cart to the right are Professor Hutton's mother, the Rector's second wife; and Lilian Leach, Alfred Hutton's fiancée.

Professor Hutton writes: 'Most country parsons farmed some small quantity of land, as a horse and trap were absolutely necessary in a scattered parish, as were a cow or two — we usually had three cows and two or three pigs. It was always cheaper to grow the hay and oats you needed than to buy. The Rectory itself had been built or rebuilt by a predecessor of my father's, a good deal earlier in the nineteenth century, and he clearly farmed a bigger acreage than my father. The glebe was extensive and had its own farmhouse nearly a mile away, which was let with the rest of the land. He had to keep cows, for there was no country milk-round. A butcher called once a week, and a fishmonger (who rarely had anything but cod), once a week or once a fortnight. The doctor, who lived seven miles away, must likewise have had some pasture of his own, as he did his rounds either on horseback or in a gig. So necessary was a little land in the nineteenth century that, under the Ecclesiastical Leases Act of 1842, which made it possible to let the glebe and farm buildings for farming purposes, it was forbidden to let the Rectory and the ten acres of the glebe most convenient to it. Kilvert, in his Diary (May 6th, 1870), records finding the Rector of Newchurch in Radnorshire castrating his lambs with the help of his daughters. Rectors in richer circumstances no doubt employed a bailiff, as did Archdeacon Grantly. Vicars, as distinct from Rectors, had no glebe; but a Vicarage in the country always had a little land with at least a paddock attached'.

27   Canon R. C. MacLeod preaching from the pulpit of Bolney Church in Sussex at about the turn of the century. Canon MacLeod was the Vicar of Mitford in Northumberland from 1897 for some forty years. He was married to Katharine Jelf, of Hastings, and was originally the vicar of Bolney, but exchanged livings with the Vicar of Mitford for the benefit of his wife's health. The present vicar of Mitford, the Reverend J. W. Stirk, to whom I am indebted for this information, writes: 'The Canon was a man of many accomplishments. He was endowed with a powerful bass voice, and people here still speak of him with great respect, but with a little fearsome awe. He was an author and composer and a very good photographer (among photographs taken by Canon MacLeod are Plates 31 and 91). Besides lecturing throughout the diocese, he entertained his parishioners on winter's evenings with magic lantern shows. The photograph of Canon MacLeod preaching was probably taken before he left Bolney, but possibly when he was making a return visit to his old parish.

28   A ruridecanal meeting at Thorpe Bassett Rectory, East Riding of Yorkshire, in 1893. Readers of the opening chapter of Charlotte Brontë's *Shirley* will recall that the young clergy of that part of Yorkshire were much given to hearty eating, and indeed ate their unfortunate landlady out of house and home. So it is perhaps not entirely coincidental that two of the photographs in this section show their subjects taking tea. Professor Hutton, who kindly sent me this photograph, and is seen near the top of the ladder in Plate 26, tells me that the photograph shows the Reverend W. Grenside, the Rural Dean (seated, left), with his two maids. On the right, holding the cream jug, is Gerard Hutton, half brother to Professor Hutton and then acting as his father's curate; and in the foreground Mr Fenton, who was Mr Grenside's curate, and lived with him, both being bachelors.

29   The Rector of Waltham in Lincolnshire having tea on the lawn in 1908. Mr W. E. R. Hallgarth, of Grimsby, who kindly sent me this photograph, remarks of it that it was 'taken in Edwardian days of ease and plenty (for parsons)'. The Latin motto on the sundial reads: 'To serve and to rule', which perhaps sums up as well as anything the attitude of the country parson of the old days towards his flock.

32

30 The Reverend W. Gooch on his horse, about 1867. Because a country parson had to look after a scattered population he could hardly manage unless he kept a horse. Often he would travel by gig, but many of his parishioners would have lived where they could not be reached by road, and an able-bodied clergyman did much of his visiting in the saddle. The incumbent of Puddingdale, Mr Quiverful, could not, it is true, afford any such luxury, but that was only because his reproductive inclinations exceeded his purse. Many a parson, like the one in this photograph, rode well and could afford to be well mounted. Often he hunted regularly, holding his place with the best of them, and at times becoming that unique product of the Church of England, the squarson.

31 The Mitford choir outing of 1911. The break is loading up at Mitford for an outing to Kelso, just over the Scottish side of the Border; the break presumably only took the party as far as Morpeth station, some three miles away, whence the railway runs through Berwick-upon-Tweed to Kelso. A journey by road, though much more direct today, would have been a difficult undertaking in horse-drawn days, since it would have involved climbing up the steep pass over the Cheviots at Carter Bar. Canon MacLeod, who took this photograph, evidently attracted some good-looking young women into his choir.

32   Dr Francis Gaman, of Caistor, Lincolnshire, about to set out on his rounds in 1905, accompanied by the curate. Miss F. R. Gaman, who kindly sent me this photograph of her father, tells me that he had a widely scattered practice in the Lincolnshire Wolds and that it was not unusual for him to have to visit patients six or eight miles away from Caistor. The smart turn-out was typical of a doctor of his day. The rug over his knees is a reminder of how little protection from the weather was afforded by a gig; this was particularly significant for a doctor, who had to turn out in all weathers.

The Doctor

The life of the doctor has probably been more changed by the coming of the internal combustion engine than that of any other character in the countryside. Before 1914 most country doctors went about their practices on horseback or in a gig. A call to a maternity case six miles away, at three in the morning, meant that the horse had to be saddled or harnessed — usually, at that hour, by the doctor himself; and afterwards the horse had to be rubbed down and fed before the doctor could get any rest himself. Not surprisingly, even before 1914, some country doctors were using cars. But the trouble with a car was that it might not get you there at all; a horse was reliable, even though it meant a great deal of work.

   Before the days of the telephone, the country doctor was at least spared unnecessary midnight calls. He could only be fetched by a messenger on foot or on horseback; and no one would walk or ride five miles to fetch him unless his services were really needed.

33   Dr Frank Hayes Smelt, of Newent, Gloucestershire, crossing a ford during his rounds in 1910. The bridge on the left is only a footbridge, so it was necessary to drive through the stream. This photograph was taken in the summer; the ford must have been a difficult obstacle during the winter. Miss Cicely Smelt, who kindly sent me this photograph of her father, tells me that he usually kept two or three horses (as did Dr Gaman). He was the doctor in Newent for fifty-two years. When he was called out at night he usually rode, otherwise he drove, as in this photograph; in winter, if the snow was deep, he sometimes drove a sleigh. Miss Smelt adds: 'Often as children we went with him on his rounds, and would hold the horse while he visited patients.' When he could spare the time, Dr Smelt was a keen follower of the Ledbury Hounds.

The Vet

34   Albert Oscar McDowell, M.R.C.V.S. This study of a country vet was kindly sent to me by his son, Mr T. A. McDowell, who writes: 'My father was one of ten of a farmer's family in Northern Ireland. He broke away and went to Glasgow, where he qualified as a veterinary surgeon in 1901. Returning home, he set up his plate in Ballynahinch, Co. Down. Because his family were well-known locally, farmers called on his services 'for practice' in the convenient belief that, as they were helping him to learn his job, there need be no fees. Finally he settled in Gloucester, where he remained for thirty-two years. He died at the age of seventy-six, after attending five cases during that day.'

Mr McDowell adds: 'My father hunted regularly with local packs until a shoulder injury stopped him. He never failed to visit the market on market days, and he served the widest range of clients, from the humblest smallholder to the wealthiest landowner. During his career he attended to everything from a kitten to a steeplechaser. He once operated on a circus elephant tethered to a street fountain.'

The Tenantry

35   The Michaelmas due — Llandrindod Wells, on September 29th, 1913. The tenants of an estate in Radnorshire have gathered on quarter day at the Rock Park Hotel, first to pay their rents to their landlord and now, having performed that duty, to enjoy their annual dinner at his expense. Though the image of the yeoman farmer, owning the land that he worked, has for centuries been popular in English mythology, before 1914 the great bulk of agricultural land was worked, as much of it still is, on the landlord and tenant system. But even when this photograph was taken the effect of death duties was beginning to make itself felt on the great landed estates, and tenant farmers were taking the opportunity of buying in the freehold of their land. The First World War, which was about to hasten still further the inevitable changes in rural life, had already broken out before the stalwart tenantry in this photograph were able to enjoy their next annual dinner.

36, 37 When oxen were still
used to work the land. These
pictures of a team of Sussex oxen
ploughing and rolling on the
Sussex downs recall a form of
husbandry that had survived from
Roman times until the early years
of the twentieth century, when
these pictures were taken. The
plough is a turnwrest, used in
Kent and parts of Sussex since
medieval times.

Agriculture

To Thomas Hardy and his contemporaries, agriculture was not only something that had
changed little since the *Georgics;* it was also something that was unlikely to change. Hardy
put it:

> *Only a man harrowing clods*
> *   In a slow silent walk*
> *With an old horse that stumbles and nods*
> *   Half asleep as they stalk.*
> *Only thin smoke without flame*
> *   From the heaps of couch grass;*
> *Yet this will go onward the same*
> *   Though Dynasties pass.*

Yet even the past twenty-five years have brought revolutionary changes in agriculture that
the nineteenth century never guessed at. The men and women in the pictures that follow were
to prove to be almost the last practitioners of traditional forms of husbandry that had endured
since the beginning of written history.

38   Harrowing with a team of oxen at the Warren, Aldbourne, Wiltshire, in 1911. The oxen are wearing collars in place of the yokes in Plate 36. The Browns, of Aldbourne, who owned this team, were a well-known Wiltshire farming family.

39   Ploughing with horses and a single-handled Norfolk-type high gallows plough about 1880. This type of plough provided a considerable improvement in speed and productivity over the ancient ox-drawn ploughs.

40   Harrowing at Coddenham, Suffolk, in about 1890.

41   Harvesting with a crook stick and reap hook in Herefordshire in about 1900. This method of cutting the harvest was already slow and out-of-date by the time the picture was taken; nevertheless, it was the method used to feed England's growing urban population during the years of the Industrial Revolution.

42 Norfolk women-harvesters working alongside their menfolk in the fields. The elaborate precautions taken to keep the sun from their faces reflects the typical nineteenth-century view that a skin browned by the sun was unbecoming, and indeed a misfortune, in a woman.

43 Threshing with flails, in the Biblical manner, in a barn about 1900. This method was already outdated when the photograph was taken, as will be seen from Plate 45.

40

44 A mowing team at Wenham Grange, Suffolk, in 1880. In *Lark Rise to Candleford* Flora Thompson records that though the mechanical reaper was known in her childhood, it was looked upon as a farmer's toy; the scythe still did most of the work. 'The men still kept up the old country custom of choosing as their leader the tallest and most highly-skilled man amongst them, who was then called "King of the Mowers." . . . Every morning they set themselves to accomplish an amount of work in the day that they knew would tax all their powers till long after sunset. "Set yourself more than you can do, and you'll do it", was one of their maxims.'

45 Threshing at Harlington, Middlesex, with a threshing machine driven by a steam engine, in 1868. This is of interest both as an early photograph and as an early example of the mechanisation of English agriculture. In the ensuing one hundred years we can reasonably claim to have maintained the lead which pioneers such as these gave us.

41

46   A mower
sharpening his scythe
at Wilcroft,
Herefordshire, about
1890.

47   Building the rick
at Mitford,
Northumberland,
around the turn of the
century. The elaborate
knee-pads are not
merely to protect the
wearer's trousers at a
vulnerable point;
anyone who has to
spend long hours
firming the sheaves in
rick-building, or
working on a ladder
with his knees resting
against the rungs, will
be liable to suffer a
form of 'housemaid's
knee' unless he
protects his knee-caps.

48   Building the haystack at Froyle Hill, Hampshire, in about 1910. The weight of hay shifted by a single horse, and the size of the rick that the three men are building, are reminders of the amount of work that could be got through at haymaking time by muscle-power alone.

49   Haymaking in Hampshire in about 1910. It is difficult to be sure whether these two women would always have turned themselves out so immaculately for a hard day's work in the hayfield, or whether their appearance was partly governed by their knowing that they were going to be photographed. In any case, their clothes would have been uncomfortably hot for work of this kind, but the chances are that their sense of fitness demanded that they should always be dressed to this standard. One of them did not consider that their wide-brimmed hats were sufficient protection against the unbecoming effects of sunburn.

50 Dinner time for the marsh-hay mowers — a photograph taken in 1889 on the River Bure, Norfolk.

51 Milking in a Cardiganshire farmyard, 1897. Taking the milk pail to the cow, rather than the cow to the milking shed, was a common practice and often involved milking in the field; but this picture, and the one that follows, and that of Mrs Hunt, the milk-woman, (Plate 80), are reminders of how much our standards of hygiene in milk-production have improved.

52 Farmers bringing milk to the factory at Calne, Wiltshire, in about 1900. Compared with the modern method of the milk-tanker that goes round and picks up the milk, this must have been a highly uneconomic method of collection, since hardly any of these farmers is carrying more than one milk-can. The photograph is a reminder of the important role, now largely forgotten, that the donkey once played in rural transport.

53 Hampshire Down sheep with their shepherd near Stonehenge, Wiltshire, 1901. At this time there were often as many as twenty thousand sheep at Marlborough fair — and someone who remembers it tells me that no-one could sleep at night in fair-time because of the noise that the sheep made.

45

54 Norfolk shepherds with their dogs near Sandringham in about 1890. Their dress is so similar as to be almost a uniform — a common enough practice at the time among countrymen, who wished their calling to be immediately recognisable from their dress.

55 Washing sheep at Arlebrook in the Cotswolds on May 27th, 1890. The sheep are being dipped in order to wash their wool before shearing, not as a protection against flystrike. The implements that resemble polo sticks are, of course, to ensure total immersion. This photograph was sent me by the present owner of the cottage in the background, who tells me that the dip still stands. She writes: 'The sheep dip is built on a stream which bounds my garden, and it has slots in the stonework to enable an iron door to be inserted to dam the stream.'

46

56 Felling trees at Puslinch, Devon, in about 1890.

Forestry

Because the axe is among the oldest of human tools, it is reasonable to suppose that forestry was, until about the end of the era with which this book is concerned, among the least changed of human activities. The foresters in these pictures probably differ little, except in dress, and in the steel of their axe heads, from their predecessors of the Stone Age. It is only in the past fifty years, with the introduction of portable machinery, that all this has changed.

57   Hauling timber at Mollington,
Oxfordshire, in 1895. The weight of the loads
that could be carried is formidable, even
allowing for the numbers of horses used; here
four appear to be hauling, or about to haul,
the immense weight of oak on the waggon
behind them.

58   Hauling timber in Mitford Park,
Northumberland, around 1900. Here is an
even more impressive example of the weight
of timber drawn, in this case, by a single
horse. The cold weather would have made
the work easier, by keeping the ground firm.

59　The woodcutters — a calotype photograph by William Henry Fox Talbot. This print was taken from one of the earliest negatives in existence, made by Fox Talbot around 1843. The heads of the two men are blurred, because they were not able to remain absolutely still for the long exposure required, but the quality of the rest of the picture is excellent, particularly in the detail of the roof.

60　Joe Willoughby, a forester on the South Ormsby estate, Lincolnshire. He is enjoying a clay pipe after his midday meal; notice the glass bottle of cold tea on the extreme right of the picture. Mr W. E. R. Hallgarth, who sent me this picture, writes of Joe Willoughby: 'He brought up a family of twenty in a thatched cottage.'

Crafts and trades

When I was gathering together the photographs for this book I did not set out with the intention of getting one representative of the principal trades and crafts that made up the pattern of rural life between 1844 and 1914. When I had finished my collecting, however, I found that I had in fact acquired pictures covering a surprisingly wide variety of country livelihoods. A few of them are still to be found today, but many have been ironed out of existence by the flattening influences of urbanisation and the Welfare State. Craftsmen and tradesmen will also be found in such sections as forestry and agriculture.

61 John Chamberlain, pedlar, of St Neot's, Huntingdonshire, in about 1860. When this photograph was taken, John Chamberlain was about sixty-five; he died ten years later, in 1870. In the sixties he was in the habit of going round the local public houses, carrying two baske one of which contained nuts, cakes and sweets, an the other small packets of seeds. He had a patter which went: 'Any gentleman want any carrot see onion seeds, parsnip seeds, lettuce seeds, parsley seeds, radish seeds, or any Windsor fine peas? What I can't get today I'll bring another day.'

62 A spinning wheel in Merioneth, about 1870. Mr Lloyd Hughes, the county archivist of Merioneth, to whom I am indebted for this photograph, tells me that the spinning wheel is the large traditional Welsh wheel, distinct from the smaller English wheel operated by a foot pedal.

63 Robert Morvinson, carrier and shoemaker of Stallingborough, Lincolnshire, in 1857. Mr Morvinson was eighty-two when this photograph was taken; so he was born in 1775, when the United States was still a British colony, and Bonnie Prince Charlie was still alive. The picture is a fine example of early photographic portraiture.

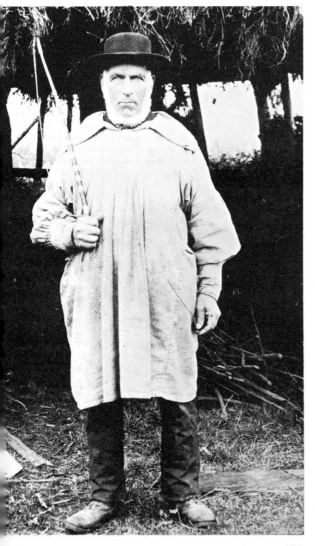

64 The carter. He carries the sign of his trade, his whip, in his right hand. The picture is also of interest for the shallow-crowned felt hat and for the carter's smock. Many tradesmen and craftsmen wore smocks, which were a kind of identifying uniform of their work, and could be matched in other counties, though the smock was also at times an indication of the wearer's locality rather than of his occupation.

65 The pump maker; a photograph taken at Lugwardine, Herefordshire, about 1900. An industrially-produced cast-iron pump is shown in Plate 7, but the much older traditional pump was made of wood, and the craftsman in this picture is engaged in the difficult task of boring out the wood with a long auger. Elmwood was used for parish pumps because it retained its strength when bored, and also withstood the effects of water.

66 The snake catcher: 'Brusher' Mills, of Gritnam Wood, in the New Forest, about 1895. Brusher Mills lived in a charcoal-burner's hut (see Plate 68) and, according to an article in *Country Life* in 1897, his only furniture was a shelf, and a large sack of beech leaves, which served him as a bed. He spent his time catching adders and other snakes, and in exhibiting and selling them at meets of hounds, fairs and horse sales. He is seen holding his two-pronged fork with which he pinned a snake to the ground; an adder would be picked up with tweezers (seen hanging in front of his waistcoat) and a grass snake by hand. The New Forest authorities paid a reward of a shilling per head for adders. Brusher Mills also supplemented his income by selling snakes to the London Zoo, and by selling clarified adder's fat, which was prized as a remedy for sprains, rheumatism, and similar ailments. It was also used (Hardy describes this in *The Return of the Native*) as a remedy for adder's bite.

67   The cobbler's family at Stratton, near Bude, Cornwall, in 1888. This seems a sizeable family to support from the takings of a single village shop, but they look prosperous enough. The Saunders' shop, on the left, was evidently confined to the taking of orders and the selling of boots and shoes; the workshop appears to have been in the stone building on the right.

68   The charcoal-burner's hut — the traditional dwelling of the trade. It was roofed with turf or heather, and lived in all the year round. This photograph of a charcoal-burner's family was taken in the New Forest in the 1890s.

69 An early promoter of pop music. In the early 90s, when this photograph was taken, before the days of radio or record-players, popular music was strictly on a do-it-yourself basis. It was performed on or round the upright piano that was part of every well-equipped front parlour. The country character shown here was a pedlar of song sheets. Though I have been unable to make out the titles of any of the songs, it is a reasonable guess that among them were some of the tunes made famous by the great Marie Lloyd.

The photograph, incidentally, is a reminder of what road surfaces were like some seventy years ago. This would have been quite a good road by the standards of its day, but very dusty in summer and distinctly muddy in winter, when the photograph was taken.

70   A door-to-door tradesman at Willersey, Gloucestershire, about 1900. We have no record of what goods he sold, but they were heavy enough to warrant the use of the wooden yoke, commonly used also for carrying milk pails on a dairy farm.

71 Gipsies with a dancing bear; Herefordshire, about 1900. Probably the true gipsies, more than any of the other country characters in this book, have withstood the 'civilising' influence of modern Britain. Getting their children to go to school remains as much of a problem as it was when this photograph was taken. But their means of livelihood have changed with the times. The exhibiting of dancing bears is now considered cruel, though keeping hens in batteries is not.

72 The blacksmith: a photograph taken about 1895. His craft is one of the few that have changed little, though he now goes in more often for cold shoeing, and he tends to travel in a truck to his customers instead of waiting for his customers to bring their horses to him. Shoeing was only part of his trade; the making and mending of iron implements, and ironwork of all kinds, were equally important.

73, 74 The smithy at Huntingdon in about 1910. Much of the interest in collecting the photographs in this book has come from the unexpected places in which some of them were found. Only too often those who have inherited early photographs, or have found them in their homes, have not appreciated their interest and importance. These two pictures, for which I am indebted to the County Archivist of Huntingdonshire, are taken from glass-plate negatives that were rescued from a back garden, where they were being used as cloches over a lettuce bed — two rows of irreplaceable negatives thrust into the earth at each side, and another row carefully laid over the top.

75   Kit and Betty Metcalfe knitting stockings outside their cottage at Gayle, near Hawes, in the North Riding of Yorkshire, in about 1900. They knitted stockings from yarn supplied by Hawes Mill; they specialised in cycling stockings, of which Kit knitted the fancy tops while his wife did the rest.

76   The costermonger, Huntingdonshire, 1910. This fine study of a costermonger's cart is another of the photographs, the plates of which were rescued after being used as cloches over a lettuce bed.

77 Johnnie in the Morning — a Gloucestershire pedlar of about 1900. His real name was Robert Hicks, but he was universally known by his nickname, and is still remembered by a few of the older inhabitants of the Tetbury area. He is thought to have come up from Bristol originally, but he worked the area of South Gloucestershire and North Wiltshire, making Tetbury his centre. His chief line of business was selling donkeys. The Gloucestershire County Records Officer, Mr Irvine Gray, has kindly sent me the following note from Mrs Kitcat, whose family once bought a donkey from him: 'Besides donkeys he sold rock-salt and silver sand, and kept black humbugs in a little box at the side of the cart to give to the children. He lived in his cart, and was always around Shipton Moyne and Westonbirt. He must have been born in 1820 or earlier.'

78   Herring curers at Seahouses, Northumberland, in the 1880s. The barrels on which they are resting are filled with salted herrings, in which there was then a brisk export trade. The women are wearing oilskin aprons to protect their skirts.

79 The warrener, Herefordshire, about 1900. A warrener was not a casual rabbit-trapper, but a man who worked a specific area of warrens, for which he usually paid rent and in which the rabbits were, as far as possible, protected from foxes and other predators.

80 The milk woman — Mrs Hunt of Calstone, Wiltshire. She went round from door to door, supplying her milk out of the tap into her customer's own jugs. The photograph is another reminder of the importance of donkeys in the rural economy before 1914.

81 A call from the miller: Warwickshire, about 1890. In *Lark Rise
to Candleford*, Flora Thompson describes the importance of gleaning
to the cottagers of her day. The grain gathered from the harvested
fields by each family was an essential item in supplementing their
diet through the coming winter. The gleaned grain was collected by
the miller, who returned it duly ground, after extracting a proportion for himself as payment. A well-filled flour sack in the corner of
the kitchen was the pride of a successful family of gleaners, though it
often meant that the farmer had deliberately not been too careful in
picking up the last of his crop.

82   The coach builder's shop; Suffolk, about 1908.
In the left foreground is a governess cart and
behind it a ralli-car. In the right foreground is
a farm cart, and beyond that another governess
cart is taking shape. Though some coach
builders had national reputations, and sold their
vehicles all over the country, the great majority of
horse-drawn vehicles were produced in small local
workshops like this one. Because of this, such
vehicles as gigs were turned out in an immense
variety of slightly differing patterns.

83   Sawyers in the saw pit at Pontrilas,
Herefordshire, about 1912. It is a sobering thought
that until quite recently all planks used in building
were sawn up by this slow and laborious method.
The sawyers worked in pairs — a top sawyer and a
bottom sawyer — and it would be likely to take a
young man many years before he worked his way
out of the pit into the superior (and much less
dusty) position of top sawyer.

84, 85 Bee-keeping at the turn of the century. Though the craft of bee-keeping has changed little over the centuries, these two pictures are of interest for the types of hive and skep. The bee-keeper in a straw boater, collecting a swarm somewhere in Herefordshire, in the year 1900, is using the traditional 'skep' shape and construction. The woman bee-keeper, probably photographed at about the same date or a little earlier, is 'telling the bees'; that is to say, she is engaged in the long-accepted practice of keeping her bees informed of her domestic affairs. She is holding a key in her right hand, as part of the ritual.

63

Grand occasions

The countryside and country towns in Victorian days were not much given to attempts at formal grandeur; that sort of thing was rightly left to the big cities. But every now and again a special occasion of national or local rejoicing produced an outburst of floral decorations in the streets; and the streets themselves were much more readily taken over for public gatherings than they are today, when they are no longer regarded as places for men and women to stroll about in, but only as highways for motor traffic.

86   A decorated arch in the High Street of Alton, Hampshire, on the occasion of the marriage of the Prince of Wales, later Edward VII, to the Danish Princess Alexandra, in 1863. The 1860s were not always marked by outbursts of popular affection for the Royal Family; indeed, the 60s and 70s were disturbed by Republican feeling and by resentment towards 'a Queen who had ceased to rule and a Prince who was contented to rule only over the fashions of the day.' But all this was forgotten when the Prince of Wales chose for his bride the beautiful Princess Alexandra of Denmark. Tennyson's

Welcome to Alexandra expressed, in an outburst of bad lines, almost all of them ending in exclamation marks, what was no doubt the popular feeling:

> *Sea-kings' daughter from over the sea,*
> > *Alexandra!*
> *Saxon and Norman and Dane are we,*
> *But all of us Danes in our welcome to thee,*
> > *Alexandra!*
> *Welcome her, thunders of fort and of fleet!*
> *Welcome her, thundering cheer of the street!*
> *Welcome her, all things youthful and sweet,*
> *Scatter the blossom under her feet!*
> *Break, happy land, into earlier flowers!*
> *Make music, O bird, in the new-budded bowers!*
> *Blazon your mottoes of blessing and prayer!*
> *Welcome her, welcome her, all that is ours!*
> *Warble, O bugle, and trumpet, blare!*
> *Flags, flutter out upon turrets and towers!*
> *Flames, on the windy headland flare!*
> *Clash, ye bells, in the merry March air!*

Bad though this seems a hundred years later, it evidently represented the feeling of the people of Alton, who put up the splendid evergreen attempt at a floral arch, which was the best that the season would allow.

Notice the muddy and dirty surface of Alton's High Street. Such surfaces were normal in the country and were much worse in the big cities, because traffic was heavier and there were therefore more horse-droppings. Hence the need for crossing-sweepers, who kept a clean track for those who wanted to cross the street. They were usually self-employed private-enterprise sweepers, not paid by the municipality, but the practice was to tip the sweeper a copper or two when you used his crossing. In busy streets they may have made quite a good thing out of it. A swept crossing can be seen in this photograph, from just beyond the lamp-post to the man on the right with his hand in his trousers pocket, but the sweeper himself does not appear to be on duty. Perhaps there were not enough people about to make it worth his while.

Curtis's *History of Alton* quotes the *Hampshire Chronicle*'s report: 'On March 14, 1863, Alton celebrated the wedding of the Prince and Princess of Wales in a very loyal and national spirit. A magnificent triumphal arch of large and noble dimensions spanned the High Street near the Market Street. The framework of timber was completely covered with trees and evergreens. On one side in large letters were the words, "Albert and Alexandra", on the other, "England and Denmark". The day was kept as a general holiday. All the Infant schoolchildren assembled at the National Schools, then paraded the High Street, and were drawn up under the arch, where they sang an anthem composed by the Misses Crowley for the occasion, and set to the tune of the National Anthem. They then marched to the Town Hall and were regaled with oranges and plum cake. Later in the day all the children of the Town, about 1000, from five years and upwards, assembled at the Railway Station, and preceded by the band, marched in procession, carrying flags and banners through the Town. They were all drawn up under the arch, where they sang the Anthem with the greatest spirit and enthusiasm. After this they were regaled with tea and cakes at the Town Hall. The principal employers of labour provided a meal for their employees.

In the evening there was a display of fireworks and a bonfire. The town was also illuminated.'

87 Celebrating Queen Victoria's Jubilee in Saxmundham, Suffolk, in 1887. By the late 1880s the Queen's popularity had surmounted the earlier waves of Republicanism, and came to a climax in the Jubilees of 1887 and 1897, by which time she was as much loved and revered as any monarch in Britain before or since.

Notice that the policeman, in the centre of the picture, with the jug in his right hand, is among the official persons who are helping to serve the populace. The season has allowed the floral arch to be more genuinely floral than that for the Prince of Wales's wedding in the previous photograph, and the day is warm enough for many of the ladies at the table on the right to have opened their parasols to protect them against the sun. A sunburnt face in a woman was, of course, a thing to be avoided at all costs if she would maintain any sort of social position.

88   It would be hard to find a more revealing example of the gulf that separated rich from poor in the English countryside than this rather forbidding picture of the preparations for an outdoor tea to the local regiment at Cusworth Hall in Yorkshire. The picture was taken in the autumn of the year 1911 and shows Lady Isabella Georgiana Katherine Battie-Wrightson, eldest daughter of the third Marquess of Exeter, about to provide afternoon tea to the men of the King's Own Yorkshire Light Infantry in the North Forecourt of her house. One glance at Lady Isabella, the commanding figure with a stick in her hand in the centre of the picture, is enough to make it unnecessary to add that only officers would be permitted to take tea with Lady Isabella herself inside the house. Indeed Lady Isabella, with her staff drawn up in battle order behind her, gives the impression that she is more prepared to repel a charge than to offer hospitality to the oncoming troops. It is interesting to see the kind of staff that was required to maintain the comforts of life in a house of this size in those days. From the left, behind the table, are a gamekeeper, a housemaid, the chauffeur, a footman, another gamekeeper, the head gardener, another housemaid, an under-butler, a kitchen maid, another under-butler, another housemaid, a footman, another housemaid, a gardener, another kitchen maid, a handyman and the butler. Further round behind the wing of the table are another housemaid, and two more gardeners. In front of the table are, besides Lady Isabella herself, the lady-in-waiting, the estate steward and the housekeeper and her assistant. Cusworth Hall, near Doncaster, was built in 1741 for William Wrightson; the East and West Pavilions were added by James Paine in 1745. There is interior plasterwork by Joseph Rose, and a fresco of the Ascension on the ceiling of the private chapel by Francis Hayman.

89   The circus comes to a country town in 1899. Perhaps this picture of the parade through the streets of Alton, Hampshire, is not quite a grand occasion in the sense of the three preceding pictures, but it was certainly an exciting day, and rather grander than any of the others, in the minds of the children of Alton, who can be seen lining the streets. Evidently it was a warm day, for three of the adult onlookers are finding it necessary to protect themselves from the sun. In George Sturt's *A Small Boy in the Sixties*, there is a good impression of what it was like for a child to stand at a front-window in a country town and watch for something unusual to go by — though Sturt was writing not of Alton but of Farnham, Surrey: 'Once, only once, I saw elephants from a travelling menagerie amble silently though swiftly along the street. More than once that window gave a good point of view of a circus procession — the clowns on their tall stilts striding by almost at one's own level. At that window I was halfway up towards the Queen of the Show on her piled-up splendour of gilt and mirrors; could look down on the backs of her piebald pony team, on her nonchalant attendants riding hand on hip. If no circus happened to go by there might be a man pushing a "Happy Family". A Happy Family was a wire cage on a long hand cart, containing all kinds of ill-assorted animals — a dog, a cat, a rabbit, a bird or two — things that one would have expected to be killing one another, and, somehow, seemed to be living together in amity.'

The building in the background of this photograph is now the Curtis Museum at Alton, to which I am indebted for this photograph among others.

90   This picture makes an agreeable footnote to the second photograph in this section. It shows one of the entries in the Jubilee Procession held at Presteigne, Radnorshire, on the 22nd June, 1897. The costumes are those of 1837, the year of Queen Victoria's Accession. To us they seem immensely remote, but to those who watched the procession the period was, of course, well within living memory. Indeed there is a strong probability that the clothes worn are not theatrical costumes or fancy dress made for the occasion, but original clothes handed down in the family; this particularly applies to the Kate Greenaway suit of the boy at the donkey's head; a suit made for him would not have fitted so badly.

91 The orchestra of the village of Mitford, Northumberland. Mitford lies some two miles west of Morpeth on the Hartburn-Bellingham road, and when this photograph was taken had a population of under two hundred — though the whole parish probably numbered some five hundred or more. It was, as it still is, largely a farming community; and in 1908, when the photograph was taken, the village must have been very proud that it had its own string orchestra. I doubt whether many English villages of its size can boast as much today. This is one of the photographs taken by Canon MacLeod, who is seen in the pulpit in Plate 27. The orchestra was formed by Miss Brenda MacLeod, and is here rehearsing in the Vicarage garden.

Leisure

In theory, at least, the people in the period covered by this book had less leisure in their lives than we do today. Hours of work were a great deal longer. Nevertheless country people seem to have found plenty of time to enjoy more things in life than work. Courting was a slower and more leisurely business; it was by no means uncommon for engagements to be protracted for several years. And it is probable that for most people the pressure of work itself was less intense. There were many more moments when it was possible to pause for a while and pass the time of day with a neighbour who happened to be walking by. There was no lack of fun and entertainment in village life, but it was mostly made by the villagers themselves and not handed out to them on a plate by broadcasting or the cinema. It is an anomaly of the 1970s that this is an age of do-it-yourself; we have had to learn to perform with our own hands many tasks for which our grandparents would have employed a specialist. Yet our grandparents were much better at providing do-it-yourself entertainment than we are.

92 Sunday-best by the bridge. This is another photograph taken by Canon MacLeod, and shows the bridge over the River Font which was known in its day as the humptyback bridge, but was replaced by the present bridge some fifty years ago. There is about the photograph a slight suggestion of 'All dressed up and nowhere to go', but the chances are that these children had walked over to the bridge expressly to pose for their photograph, in itself an exciting Sunday novelty.

93 Cricket on the lawn in the Vicarage garden at Mitford. The engaging little person with her back to the camera is, I understand, Mrs MacLeod, the Canon's wife. The children are her daughters and friends. It is clear that garden cricket, including the angle of the little girl's bat, has not changed.

94 A Sunday boating party of about 1890 on the River Tyne, below Bywell Castle. This rather looks as though the scene was posed for the photographer — or else the oarsman has forgotten to cast off forrard. Nevertheless it has about it an agreeable air of leisurely courting.

95 The wayside gossip: a carefully 'composed' photograph of 1883. This picture is notable for two things — its excellent photographic quality; and the obvious artificiality of the group. I suspect that they dressed up for the occasion and posed against the carefully chosen background in order to provide the photographer with the kind of result that could be regarded, in its day, as nearly as good as a painting. For this was still in the phase when photographers were trying to imitate painters, and painters were attempting to copy the detailed accuracy of the photograph. In spite of its artificiality, however, the picture has managed to preserve for us something of the unhurried pace of life in the 1880s; a sense of leisure and permanence that vanished forever from the English scene in August, 1914. In some of the later photographs in this book, taken in the early years of the twentieth century, the sense of impending disaster can already be detected; but here, on a summer day in 1883, the world is secure and permanent; England is set in her ways like the stars in their courses; and it is clearly the will of Providence that things shall go on like this for ever.

96   The Curtis family playing croquet in their garden at Alton, Hampshire, in 1865. I regard this as one of the most charming of all the photographs I have been able to discover. It was taken just over one hundred years ago; it shows that our ancestors really did wear these incredibly hot and stuffy clothes on a warm summer's day, and even tried to be mildly athletic in them; and it preserves, in the prolonged minute during which the slow plate of the camera was being exposed, the almost sacred spirit of unity in the mid-Victorian middle-class family. This photograph comes from the Curtis Museum in Alton, which was founded by the father of the family, Dr Curtis, the benign figure seated on the right, with a white bushy beard. The first member of the Curtis family came to Alton in the early years of the eighteenth century. This man founded a dynasty of local doctors, who provided the town of Alton with medical care for four generations. A grandson of the first Curtis in Alton attended Jane Austen when she lived at Chawton.

97   The Potato Race in the paddock of Hilmarton Vicarage, Wiltshire, about the turn of the century. After sixty years the *dramatis personae* in this familiar village event have acquired a certain charm and even dignity. But it is easy to see how strongly the Curtis family in the preceding photograph would have disapproved of the ungainly dress and antics of these young ladies; it is even possible to discern that some of them actually have legs beneath their skirts! The scene, in reality, could hardly have been more respectable; several of the characters are members of the landed, titled and official classes; but to the Curtis family they would have appeared shockingly decadent and *fin-de-siècle*.

98 A seaside picnic at the turn of the century. This large party, who had probably come in a horse-drawn charabanc, were photographed behind an old cottage by the shore at Northcott Mouth, in Cornwall, about the year 1900. The owner of the cottage catered for picnickers by providing them with tables and chairs and hot water, but they brought their own food. Judging by the expression on the face of the little boy who turned to face the camera, the tea provided was pretty good. The umbrella on the chair does not necessarily mean that it was a wet day. Umbrellas were frequently used as parasols in summer, as can be seen in the photograph of the circus passing through Alton (Plate 89).

99 A picnic party in Breconshire in 1896. The members of the party were staying at Llanwrtyd Wells and were driving up the old drover's road beyond Abergwesyn. The break is well maintained and a smart turn-out, but the ponies seem remarkably small to draw such a load in hilly country. On this occasion the picnickers seem to be taking their pleasure rather seriously; only the dog is thoroughly enjoying himself.

100   The Morris men of Northill in Bedfordshire in about 1910. I
had some doubts about including this photograph because Morris
men still keep up their traditions today and there is not much to dis-
tinguish them from those of sixty years ago. But Thomas Hardy, in
his account of the mummers at Christmas on Egdon Heath in *The
Return of the Native*, remarks that the genuine survival of a tradition
can always be distinguished from the modern revival because in the
latter the performers will appear enthusiastic, whereas in the former
they will seem to be carrying out their annual task out of a sense of
dreary obligation. The performers in this photograph appear to
qualify as a genuine survival under the Hardy rule.

Sport

Ever since the Normans came, sport has occupied a curiously ambivalent position in the social structure of English country life. It has been both a principal cause of friction between rich and poor, and at the same time one of the common interests drawing all good countrymen together. During the period covered by this book the social layers were still rigidly defined, not yet having been melted by the solvent of two world wars, and sport was still playing its dual role of divider and uniter that began when the New Forest was cleared of peasant farmers to provide hunting country for Norman nobles. The villagers of the nineteenth and early twentieth centuries poached the landowner's pheasants and salmon and cursed him when they were caught for it; but they said 'Good morning, Master,' to him with the greatest good humour when they met the same man at a meet of the local hounds.

101 A shoot at Old Riffams, near Little Baddow, Essex, in 1905. I have been able to find out very little about the people taking part in this shoot. The bearded character in the background is almost certainly a beater, but it is difficult to type-cast any of the others. Mr P. A. Gouldsbury, the secretary of the Gamekeepers' Association, kindly sent this photograph to an Essex gamekeeper with a long memory in the hope that he might recognise some of the faces, but he has only been able to reply: 'In my opinion it is a late-season shoot, probably by farmers and keepers, maybe head-keepers from neighbouring estates. The dress is not up to the standard of the big shooting parties of that date.'

By today's standards, the dress of the six guns in the front row is as immaculate as their bearing is military; big-shoot standards must have been high indeed. Spartan qualities were no doubt needed; taking high birds while wearing a stiff razor-edge collar must have been distinctly uncomfortable.

102   A young angler on the river Font in Northumberland. This is another of the photographs taken by Canon MacLeod, the vicar of Mitford, in the late nineteenth and early twentieth centuries.

103   Coursing in Coquetdale — a photograph taken by the local historian, David Dippie Dixon. In the north of England many of the miners still keep dogs of this kind, as their grandfathers and great-grandfathers did before them. Few modern photographers, however, could rival the skill of this picture in capturing the tautness and concentration of its subjects.

104   A meet of the Morpeth hounds at Mitford, Northumberland, in 1911. This photograph was taken by Canon R. C. MacLeod, who was the vicar of Mitford for nearly forty years. The Churchillian figure on the left is the old squire, watching hounds about to move off after what was evidently a lawn meet at his house. Hunting has changed so little in dress and outward appearance that photographs of meets fifty years ago frequently look little different from those taken last week; I chose this picture because the clothes of the squire's ladies help to date it; but apart from them, nothing has changed. When this photograph was taken the Master was Captain F. B. Atkinson, who held that office for the remarkable stretch of thirty-five years. He and the vicar must have seemed to Mitford men and women to represent in their persons the continuity of English rural life.

105 The falconer; Major C. Hawkins Fisher, of Stroud, Gloucestershire. Major Fisher contributed a number of articles on falconry to *Country Life* in the 1890s and was besides an all-round sportsman, holding for several years the championship of the Toxophilite Society. This photograph was published in *Country Life* of November 2nd, 1901, on the occasion of his death at the age of seventy-five. The same issue carried his last article on falconry, written just before his death, in which he described a curious mishap that had occurred to him while he was out with a young passage falcon on the Wiltshire downs. During the flight he had left his mare unattended, knowing that she was accustomed to being left alone and untethered on the open downland, but when he returned, the mare had vanished. He finally found her swimming about with obvious pleasure in a dewpond. He complained that apart from the difficulty of getting the mare out of the pond, the saddle was too wet to ride on during the journey home.

106 A Herefordshire poacher of about 1870. This remarkable old photograph has come down to us as being that of a poacher, but perhaps it should be taken with a grain of salt. In appearance the man looks as though he might well have been a poacher, but it is not altogether likely that a real poacher would have been prepared to pose for his photograph, gun in hand, standing at the corner of an identifiable field over which he was not entitled to shoot. The explanation may be that this is an example of the kind of early photograph that was taken in imitation of a painting, and was posed for the photographer by some blameless individual who may never have been up before the local Bench in his life.

107 A gamekeeper in the 1840s. If this section would have been incomplete without the poacher, it would have been even less complete without the gamekeeper. But here is no ordinary gamekeeper. It is the gamekeeper at Lacock Abbey, Wiltshire, and the picture was taken by William Henry Fox Talbot, who invented at Lacock the negative-positive process on which modern photography is based. This may be, therefore, the first photograph of a gamekeeper ever taken. A fuller account of the Lacock Abbey photographs will be found in the introduction.

The Inn

108 The Star Inn at Alfriston in Sussex. A photograph taken in about 1910. So much has been written by Victorian and Edwardian novelists and poets about the English inn that it is unnecessary to provide any description of what this charming little hostelry, and the many like it all over the country, offered to visitors in the peaceful years when the photograph was taken. It is true that many of the inns are little changed today; but if a modern visitor to the Star could suddenly be switched back in time to 1911, what would strike him most would be the silence of the streets — at night he would have found it, in the words of the modern Cockney, 'So quiet he couldn't sleep.'

The Star at Alfriston happily remains one of the finest specimens of an ancient English inn. It was originally founded in the thirteenth century, but the surviving building dates from about 1450. The inn's curious sign, unchanged today, probably represents the star of Bethlehem, for although the crest of the Innholder's Company — a sixteen-pointed star — was in common use, the date of this inn is much earlier than that of the Company.

109 Delivering the beer at the Rising Sun, Billericay, Essex. The waggon, which bears a close resemblance to the covered waggon of the American pioneer or of the South African voortrekker, is a much less impressive vehicle than the horse-drawn brewer's drays that still grace the streets of London and other cities, but that is no doubt because it was a normal workaday means of getting beer from the brewer to the publican and not intended as an upholder of prestige. Notice the bucket hanging below the rear axle. It was common for the driver of draught horses to carry a day's feed for his horses, and possibly water as well, when he set out in the morning. If he did not actually carry water, then he would carry a bucket for his horses to drink from. Horses out of the stable were, of course, fed from nosebags, which were a common enough sight in the streets of London even as late as 1939. An impatient horse, feeding from a nosebag, would throw his head about and spill a little of his feed; so wherever a horse was feeding, there you would find a small attendant gathering of pigeons and other birds taking advantage of the horse's bounty. The notices over the door and the archway tell us that the Rising Sun provides 'Good Accommodation for Commercials,' and that Messrs Vincent and Philp, Veterinary Surgeons, will attend here on Mondays and Fridays.

110 Round the herring cart. The housewives of Newcastle have little time for the elegant courtesies of Hesba Stretton's morning call on her baker; they are looking for a good tea for their menfolk when they return in the evening. This excellent photograph was taken by David Dippie Dixon, the historian of Coquetdale. I do not know the date, but would guess about 1880.

Shops and shopping

Surprisingly enough, the village shop has proved to be one of the most enduring of all rural institutions. It is one of the few things left in the English village that not only looks much the same as it did fifty years ago, but even whose smell is unchanged. Those whose memories go back far enough tell me that the smell of the English village shop is just the same now as it was before 1914. I have often tried to work out what that delicious smell is compounded of; oatmeal, bacon, tea, tobacco, paraffin and tarry fire-lighters form a permanent background, I think, with overtones of apples, brussels sprouts and spring onions according to the season.

   The social background to shopping, however, has changed beyond recognition. Before 1914 the important thing was to get the custom of the big house and the rectory. That would provide the shopkeeper with an assured income, even if the inhabitants of both those distinguished establishments were often a little slow in paying. Sales to other members of the rural community provided the jam on the shopkeeper's bread and butter. Frequently the retailer would call daily, or on regular days, at the houses of his more important customers in order to find out what they wanted; if he had left them to call at his shop, they might have taken their custom elsewhere. The idea that anyone with pretensions to being 'carriage folk' should actually carry his purchases away with him was, of course, unheard of. The personal shopper placed his order; delivery was part of the tradesman's job.

111 Morning salutation: Hesba Stretton at Mary York's in New Street, Wellington, Shropshire. The exact date of this photograph is not known, but from Hesba Stretton's dress it was probably the early 1870s. The Post Office Directory of Shropshire for the year 1865 shows Mary York as keeping a baker's shop; to judge from the jars in the photograph, she evidently sold sweets as well.

Hesba Stretton, though her name is no longer widely known, was a highly successful authoress in her day. Her real name was Sarah Smith, but under her pen name she wrote *Jessica's First Prayer*, an improving work that describes a poor young girl's discovery of religion. It first appeared in *The Sunday at Home* in 1866, and was issued in book form a year later, with results that would still make any publisher pale with envy. It sold one and a half million copies, and it was translated into every European language and most Asiatic and African languages as well. Hesba Stretton was born in 1832; if she was forty when the photograph was taken (and she does not look more), that dates it at 1872.

112　Shopping in a market town in the 1880s. This photograph of the New Road, now known as the High Street, of Aylesbury, Buckinghamshire, was taken between 1883 and 1885. The road itself was not all that old — hence its name — having been originally built in 1826. It is now part of A.41. Most of the shops shown have recently been pulled down. The three-wheeler pram, with its wooden wheels and no springs, probably looked a little old-fashioned when this photograph was taken.

113　A quiet afternoon's shopping in Calne, Wiltshire. Buckeridge, on the right, was a well-established grocer; Telling, on the left, was a saddler. At least one saddler was to be found in every small town; their virtual disappearance is one of the most marked changes in the pattern of shops in the past century. The plump little pony and the gig in the foreground are roughly the equivalent of the Mini-Minor of today. Sometimes the young lady would be driven by a groom or coachman; but if she wanted to carry a passenger, as here, she would drive herself. The man with the smart sideburns is evidently a shopkeeper being polite to a customer; he has a pencil behind his ear.

114 The baker's cart at Bala, Merioneth, possibly in the 1880s. This baker's round must have been confined to a comparatively small area, or he could not have served it with a donkey and cart. Most country bakers used a pony or light horse, because they had to cover a considerable distance.

115 Mr Pearson's saddler's shop in the village of Washbrook, Suffolk, in about 1890. In connection with the opposite photograph I remarked that nearly every small town had its saddler's shop; so did many villages, though in this Suffolk village most of the display is harness for heavy and light draught horses, no doubt mainly for agricultural use. Notice that the little girl in her grandfather's gig is being allowed to 'drive' — that is to say, hold the reins just behind grandfather's hands. Being allowed to drive a pony is one of the delights of which modern children have been deprived. With a trusted pony it was often possible to leave the reins entirely in the child's hands. One of my own earliest recollections, during the First World War, is of being given the reins by my grandmother and of the pony 'running away'.

116 A Christmas display at the shop of Gates and Company, Alton, Hampshire, in about 1890. This very elaborate display can hardly have been taken in when the shop was closed at night. Most of it must have been left up until it was sold, or until the end of Christmas. Notice that besides the hares outside the first-floor windows there are three boars' heads over the name of the shop. In addition to all the usual goods offered by Gates and Company's 'noted meat shop', Mr Gates, who is on the left in the picture, seems to have sold pickles and other condiments; notice the jars in the left-hand window.

117 A grocer and draper's shop in the village of
Great Baddow, Essex. The interesting thing about
this shop is that it is a *wholesale* grocer's. Such
shops were a necessary part of distributive business
when goods travelled by rail and by horse transport.
They provided a chain of depots from which other
villages, perhaps further from a railway, could
draw their supplies. This shop would certainly have
encouraged retail trade with local customers as well.

Fairs and markets

118, 119   Castle Street Fair, at Farnham, Surrey, in about 1883. There is a good description of this Fair in George Sturt's *A Small Boy in the Sixties*.'In my earliest years the Fair was already in full blast o' mornings when I woke up for the day. Already could be heard unwonted noises from down in the street; and one had not to look long to see down below a hurry of strange sights — a herd of black Welsh bullocks coming over from Blackwater Fair, a dishevelled gang of gypsies, a flock of sheep thronging the street from side to side, sheep dogs rushing and barking to keep slow sheep on the move and in order, a little group of farmers (not, as on market days, in their best clothes), a show cart, a dirty gig or two, unkempt mumpers quarrelling and spoiling for a fight at public-house doors, hard-faced travelling women with sticky-looking brown hair; and at times, as if all this straggling, careless, swearing, jostling crowd were not enough, along the street would come folk who gave no other heed, a shady-looking fellow — a horse coper — running a frightened horse for sale. No other heed? Not quite so, either. Anybody with a whip, and there were many — gyp, farmer, half-and-half — was liable to crack it loudly for the fun of frightening the horse into a faster trot. And above the yells, the bleating, the clatter of horse-hooves, and loud chatter and other nameless noises, came the thin toot of toy trumpets bought at a stall, the cries of showmen, the bang of beetle, driving into the road the stakes for some cokernut shy or still unfinished stall.'

For a contrast to these photographs turn to Plate 137, the same street on an ordinary day.

120 Lincoln Horse Fair in 1905. Horse copers were not always noted for their strict honesty, and anyone who wanted to avoid being done on such an occasion had to keep his wits about him, and have an eye for a horse. Most of these 'hairies' would have found new homes on farms, or between the shafts of carts and waggons of the heavier sort.

121 Barnard Castle Market, Co. Durham, around the turn of the century. Notice all the parked gigs, wagonettes and carts up both sides of the street on the left. On Market Day the congestion caused by parking must have been only slightly less than it is today. Compare this with Plates 141 and 142, which also show the parking problem in Barnard Castle, and it will be seen that the average modern motorist's conviction that he has a natural right to leave his car in the street while he goes shopping is inherited from ancestors who, for many centuries, enjoyed and exercised that right. Our present difficulties are two-fold: the unmanageable pace and bulk of motor traffic; and our misconception of the purpose of streets, which we regard as motor-highways rather than as places for the local people to use and enjoy. Traffic congestion is, of course, a problem as old as urban life; the Romans had laws to deal with it, including one that limited the hours when heavy goods vehicles could use the streets. But former ages were helped by the fact that the parking of horse-drawn vehicles was to some extent self-limiting; after a time you had to go back to feed not the meter but the horse.

122 The Old Market, St Ives, Huntingdonshire, in 1890. The street is a principal thoroughfare through the town, but it is plain that the people in the picture have no doubts about its proper purpose: it is a place to stand and gossip, and to buy and sell. Some of today's county surveyors have something to learn from this photograph; too many of them think that all that matters in a street is to keep cars moving along it. Not long ago I heard a county surveyor, at a public meeting, declare that he didn't give a damn for the town — his only concern was to get the coast-bound traffic through it.

123 A big attraction at Melford Fair, Suffolk, in about 1908. This was a bioscope show, an early form of cinematograph. The notice on the right 'They would have harem skirts!' bears a distinct family resemblance to the film posters of today, with their unvarying suggestion that the picture advertised is a good deal more daring and improper than it turns out to be, once you have paid your money. The fantasy 'Battle in the Air' preceded by only a few years the reality of the Zeppelins.

124 Driving pigs to market down High Street, Deritend, North Warwickshire (now a part of Birmingham), in 1903. In most places this was the normal way of getting livestock to market. If the beasts held up the traffic, that was too bad for the traffic. Even today the Law is on the side of the man who drives his beasts along the Queen's Highway, provided that he takes reasonable care.

125　The annual Statute Fair at Wisbech in Cambridgeshire, about 1908. Nearly all these hopeful faces, staring up at the photographer, are servants waiting to be hired. Their possessions are in the tin trunks and boxes piled up on the right.

The Labour Exchange and the 'Sits. Vac.' column in the local paper have superseded the Statute Fair as a way of finding jobs or employees, but it was a national habit until 1914. There is a good account of a Fair of this kind in Thomas Hardy's *Far from the Madding Crowd*. Gabriel Oak is looking for a job and goes to the Statute or Hiring Fair in Casterbridge, the county town of Wessex.

'At one end of the street stood from two to three hundred blithe and hearty labourers waiting upon Chance — all men of the stamp to whom labour suggests nothing worse than a wrestle with gravitation, and pleasure nothing better than a renunciation of the same. Among these, carters and waggoners were distinguished by having a piece of whip-cord twisted round their hats; thatchers wore a fragment of woven straw; shepherds held their sheep-crooks in their hands; and thus the situation required was known to the hirers at a glance.

'In the crowd was an athletic young fellow of somewhat superior appearance to the rest — in fact his superiority was marked enough to lead several ruddy peasants standing by to speak to him inquiringly as to a farmer, and to use "Sir" as a finishing word. His answer always was, — "I am looking for a place myself — a bailiff's. Do ye know of anybody who wants one?"'

The Post

Looked back on with hindsight, the development of the national postal services in the nineteenth century stands out as one of the most beneficent changes that ever affected English country life. It brought letters from family and friends, and it brought newspapers, books, and all kinds of goods light enough to be sent by post, to people in remote country districts who had hitherto been largely deprived of these advantages; and at the same time the changes that the postal services brought to the countryside were in no way destructive. The motor-car in recent decades has brought an equal, and equally sudden, increase in the communications available to country people; but the internal-combustion engine has brought with it at least as much destruction as it has brought advantages — as is made clear on some of the other pages in this book, which show what country life was like before the coming of the car.

The photographs that follow depict the country postman as the revered and respected citizen that he undoubtedly was; and they reflect also something of his own sense of importance, and his satisfaction in the job that he was doing.

126   The post-office staff at Shifnal, Shropshire, in 1900. Dan Hall, the Postmaster, is in the shop doorway. Next to him is Lizzie Hall, his elder daughter. His younger daughter (whose Christian name I do not know) is on the far left. The postman in the doorway on the right is William Bludd, and the messenger boy in front of him is young Henry Harris. Sitting on the handle of the truck is Dan Hall junior, the Postmaster's son. Harry Roberts is the postman behind the tricycle; Bert Bailey has his hand on the handlebars. The postman at the horses' head is Arthur Bailey. The young

man sitting on the basket, with the stick in his hand, is the son of William Bludd. Unfortunately I do not know the names of the other members of the team, and I do not know the names of the dogs; that is a pity, because the dogs were unpaid members of the Post Office staff and accompanied the postmen on their rounds.

The County Record Office at Shrewsbury, who have preserved this excellent photograph, obtained the names of the people in it from Mr H. Harris, a former inhabitant of Shifnal. Mr Harris also supplied the following information: 'The postman with the trap lived in Aston Street, Shifnal. He went to Newport each night, and each morning brought the mail from Newport in the trap'. Notice that two of the postmen are carrying walking sticks. Many of them were also cobblers. They had workshops at the end of their rounds, and delivered mail on the way out to these shops. Presumably they collected repairs on the way out, and delivered them on the way back.

When this photograph was taken the Post-Office had, perhaps, reached the peak of its efficiency and cheapness, and it was obviously regarded by its employees as a highly desirable service, as is clear from the extent to which sons followed fathers. 1900 was, of course, a long way from the first days of Roland Hill's penny post, which was introduced in 1840. At that time a letter of up to half an ounce was carried for one penny, with a further penny for the next half ounce; after that it was two-pence for each additional ounce. Postage stamps were introduced at the same time, although the original stamps, though painted with adhesive on their backs, had to be cut out with scissors; per-foration was not introduced until 1854. By 1897, just before this photograph was taken, the weight that could be posted for one penny was raised to four ounces, and a regular delivery was organised to every house in the United Kingdom — an achievement that still seems staggering today. Notice that although this shop was the post office (the words are displayed in the frame just below the first-floor windows), it was also, and perhaps primarily, a booksellers, stationers and printers. The notice over the door tells us that it was also the depot of the Christian Knowledge Society.

127　The postman at Althorpe in Lincolnshire. The Post-Office in this village in 1905, when the photograph was taken, was, to judge from the braces in the window, part of an outfitter's shop, and not in the general store, as would be more common today in a small village. The enamel notice above the letterbox reads 'Post Office for Money Order, Savings Bank, Parcel Post & Insurance and Annuity Business.'

95

128 Arthur Prime, the Head Postman at Needham Market and District Post-Office, Suffolk, in 1907. Wearing the lower three buttons of the tunic unbuttoned was evidently *de rigueur*, and was perhaps intended to display the embossed waistcoat buttons and the watch chain. One glance at Mr Prime's face is enough to assure us that he would not have posed for his photograph with his jacket undone, if this could ever have been thought to be slovenly. Mr Prime wears five long service stripes, as does Mr William Bludd in Plate 126.

129 The Parcel Post in Berkshire in 1905. Though this photograph has a genuine air about it, and looks no more posed than was necessary for the exigencies of a slow-speed camera and plate, it was in fact taken with the intention that it should be used in an advertisement. The parcel being delivered is a packet of Sutton's seeds, and the recipient who has posed with the postman was a member of the Sutton family.

130 The Postmaster at Astley in Warwickshire off duty. He is the magisterial figure seated on the right. Unfortunately the photographer has left us no record of his name; but note that he is described as the Postmaster, not as a retired Postmaster. Before the days of universal old-age pensions, men and women who were able to do so went on working until much later in life than our modern sixty-five and sixty, and were often all the better for it.

Public affairs

Because this book deals with the days before television and before the Welfare State, public services and public life were both more local and more intimate than they are today.

131 Electioneering at Old Bolingbroke, Lincolnshire, in 1911. Though it is obviously a posed photograph, taken on behalf of Lieutenant-Colonel (later Sir) Archibald Weigall, who was Member of Parliament for the Horncastle division of Lincolnshire from that year until 1920, it nevertheless has in it much of the flavour of electioneering in the days when the candidate's own personality, and his ability to put on a good show in the village hall, counted — and not the television performance of his party leader. This is yet another instance (see also Plates 52 and 80) of the importance of donkeys in village life before 1914; though the humour of using a donkey to extol the virtues of a parliamentary candidate can hardly have been lost on the electors.

132 Main water comes to Highworth, Wiltshire. The citizens of Highworth have turned out on August 4th, 1904, to witness the astonishing spectacle of a jet of high pressure water playing high in the air over Highworth's Market Square. So far as they were concerned, the jet age had come to Highworth. A water tower was constructed at Reddown, above Highworth, and the cost of this, together with the laying of water mains, came to the considerable sum of £3,352. For a comparatively small extra charge every householder in Highworth would now be able to have main water on tap in his own home; and what is more, water at sufficient pressure, as the photograph makes plain, to reach a tank in the attic of his own house without further pumping.

Before this memorable day, a few of the inhabitants of Highworth would have had water storage tanks in the roofs of the houses; but the water would have had to be laboriously pumped by hand from the well in the garden each time the tank needed filling. For most people water was simply drawn in a bucket from the pump as and when it was needed (see Plate 7).

Roads and traffic

I have chosen this as a convenient title for a group of photographs, but by modern standards it might have been more appropriate to call it 'Roads and the absence of traffic'. Through all these photographs, and among several others in different sections (see pages 66 and 91), runs the same theme: the road is the centre of village life, the place where neighbours stop and chat, where children play in safety, and where hens can cluck in peace and dignity. It is not, as it has since become, a petrol-drenched highway that, during busy hours, divides the villagers on one side of the street from their former neighbours on the other.

133   Those who have driven along the London-Chelmsford-Colchester road in recent years, and remember the left-and-then-right jink that the road makes through the village of Kelvedon, will find in this photograph, of the same stretch of road running through Kelvedon in 1860, the most damning of all evidence of what the motor-car has done to village life. Here, on a sunny morning a century ago, the good people of Kelvedon are talking business or discussing the state of the nation; anyone who tried to stand and gossip in the same place today would be dead or maimed within three minutes; if by a miracle he survived that long he would probably be fined for jay-walking or for obstructing the traffic. As it happens, the dusty surface on which these top-hatted gentlemen are standing so confidently is an ancient Roman road. It echoed to the disciplined tramp of the legionaries' feet on the way to Camulodunum centuries before the English built their pleasant village along its sides. For generation after generation, for close on two thousand years, this bend in the Roman road to Colchester remained little changed. Only the ingenuity of twentieth-century man has succeeded in sacrificing the peace of Kelvedon in the name of the contemporary religion of car-worship.

134, 135 The village street of Mitford, Northumberland, in the opening years of the twentieth century: above, on a quiet day; and below on a day of heavy traffic. It was the annual practice in Mitford for farmers to bring their sheep down to be washed in the river Font, in a pool just below the bridge, and it is probable that these sheep were waiting for that purpose.

136 Buckingham Street, Aylesbury, in 1884. Once again the road (now part of A.41) is being used for what was originally felt to be part of its proper purpose — as a place for standing about and talking. The shadows make it plain that the absence of traffic in this market-town scene is not due to the photographs being taken late in the evening or early in the morning. This is just the normal traffic-density at a fairly busy time. The parking problem is not intense; one cart, from which the horse has been removed and led into a stable at the back of one of the houses. The peace and quiet is certainly not because the picture was taken on a Sunday, or the tradesman in the foreground would not have been wearing his workaday apron.

The chicken in this picture, like the one in the riddle, clearly wants to get to the other side, and for the nursery days of our ancestors the riddle must have had a suitably pointless point. Now it has none at all, for chickens no longer cross roads. Any hen that tried to cross this street today could only have suicide in mind.

In the past decade or two a number of the buildings in Buckingham Street, Aylesbury, have been taken down and replaced by such improvements as a bus garage, a supermarket and some office blocks. But that is not necessarily a bad thing. Most of the houses in this scene of 1884 were themselves built to replace earlier dwellings that had outlived their usefulness.

137 Castle Street, Farnham, Surrey, in the 1880s. Compare this photograph with the same street at its busiest moment in the year (Plates 118 and 119). It is difficult to be sure whether the tricycle in the right foreground belongs to the boy or to the young woman — probably to the latter, or she would not have been exposing so much leg. But parents in the '80s can have had no qualms about letting their children ride bicycles or tricycles in the town streets. None of these horse-drawn vehicles looks as though it is likely to run anyone down. The three furthest away are tradesmen's carts of one kind or another; but the gig coming towards the camera is quite an elegant turnout, driven by a uniformed servant in white breeches and cockaded silk hat.

Photography is still sufficiently unusual to attract attention. The taker of this photograph is being stared at earnestly by the white-aproned saddler outside the saddler's shop on the right, just beyond the tricycle.

103

138 Huntingdon Street, St Neots, in about 1910. The star of this picture is undoubtedly little Tommy, and the thing to notice about his performance is that he is standing in the road; not just walking across it, but actually standing in it, because it strikes him as a nice place to be. And little Tommy's Mum, over on the pavement with his kid sister, isn't even shouting at him to come back on the pavement at once before he gets killed. Lucky little Tommy, who spent his childhood in the days when the road was a place to play conkers on, and not just a place where you had to avoid being killed. The notice on the gates next door to the Globe Inn says: 'Good stabling'. This was commonly to be found outside country pubs before 1914 (I can only think of one, the Vauxhall Inn near Tonbridge, that still displays it). It was the equivalent in its day of: 'Parking in rear of premises.'

   The sign of the Globe Inn carries a legend that I can just make out with a magnifying glass on the original photograph. It reads, a trifle sententiously:

   Assist the struggler, thy friend and brother, And through the World we'll help each other.

139 New Road, Calne, Wiltshire, at about the turn of the century. Modern motor traffic may have brought disadvantages to both town and country life, but this typical road of its time reminds us of one of the advantages. On a wet day it must have been impossible to cross any normal road without getting one's feet muddy, and probably also dirtied with horse droppings. In busy town streets the crossing was kept reasonably clean by a crossing sweeper. (See Plate 86.)

140   The end of the muddy road of Victorian England. With the development of the motor car in the early years of the twentieth century, the tarring of roads, to prevent dust in summer and mud in winter, became more and more widespread. This picture of a road gang tarring was taken in the village of Fullstow, Lincolnshire, in 1910. In addition to the examples of ordinary untarred roads in the preceding pages of this section, there is a good example of the muddiness of an untarred road in the picture of a pedlar of song-sheets (Plate 69).

A good impression of what the roads were like in the days of horse traffic is given by Flora Thompson in *Lark Rise*. She is describing the main road that ran to Oxford from a road-junction near Lark Rise, the hamlet where the Laura of her story was born.

'Up and down went the white main road between wide grass margins, thick berried hedgerows and overhanging trees. After the dark mire of the hamlet ways, even the milky-white road surface pleased them (the children she was writing about), and they would splash up the thin, pale mud, like uncooked batter, or drag their feet through the smooth white dust until their mother got cross and slapped them.

'Although it was a main road, there was scarcely any traffic for the market town lay in the opposite direction along it, the next village was five miles on, and with Oxford there was no road communication from that distant point in those days of horse-drawn vehicles. . . . People were saying that far too much money was being spent on keeping such roads in repair, for their day was over.'

Flora Thompson was writing, of course, of the time when the railways had drawn all the traffic off the turnpike roads, just as the roads have now drawn the traffic off the railways. I wonder how many of those who look through these pages will live to see the day when the turn of fortune's wheel draws the traffic to some more practical form of transport and leaves the roads, on which we now spend so much of our national income, once again empty and deserted.

141, 142 The parking problem hits Barnard Castle, Co. Durham. I was particularly glad to discover these two pictures in the City Library of Newcastle upon Tyne because the parking problem of horse-drawn days, though it undoubtedly existed, does not often come out in contemporary photographs. These pictures, taken on market day, show only half the problem; the other half, which would otherwise be between the shafts, has been led away to some of the Good Stabling referred to in Plate 138. Parking in horse-drawn days had one peculiar advantage: a well-trained horse would take himself off and wait for his driver at a more convenient point if he knew the area well enough. It was a commonplace sight to see the horse of a milk cart or baker's cart move on, without further orders, to the next house on the run as soon as the roundsman got down to make his delivery.

The countryman on wheels: Railways

143   Bulkington Station, Warwickshire, in 1890. Though the railways brought great changes — and great improvements — to country life in the nineteenth century, they brought these changes without destroying the fabric of what had gone before. Rural England at the peak of the railway age was not greatly different from rural England at the end of the coaching era. And once the railways were built, they themselves became part of the unchanging pattern. To the lay eye, this country station and signal box are little different from a hundred others to be found all over England until the present day, or at least until Beeching's Purge. Only the costumes of the three women, and the trade names in some of the advertisements, suggest that this photograph was taken in 1890 and not in 1960. In fact Bulkington station, opened on December 1st, 1847, was closed as long ago as March 18th, 1931. The building stands today, though the platform has been demolished, and the outline of the letters of the name can still be seen. In the 1890s Bulkington boasted eleven trains a day: six locals from Rugby to Stafford, and five in the opposite direction. But many more trains passed through the station without stopping, for this is the main line from Euston to the North.

The countryman on wheels: Buses

Perhaps the greatest single change that has come about in rural life in the last half-dozen decades is the increase in individual mobility. Before 1914 it was by no means rare for men and women to live their whole lives without seeing anything of the world beyond the boundaries of their own parish. This was not because it was too difficult to get about, but because for many people it was too expensive; or at least because they had no motive to justify the expense. Journeys by train often involved an expensive journey by road to reach the nearest station; and only those who were comfortably off could afford their own horse-drawn vehicle. Even Mrs Quiverful, the parson's wife of Puddingdale, had to beg a lift on the cart of a friendly neighbour in order to reach the cathedral town of Trollope's Barchester for that vital interview with the she-Bishop, Mrs Proudie. The very term, carriage folk, reminds us that those who could afford the luxury of a carriage were a class apart. Buses, of course, carried all and sundry cheaply, but their range was short before the coming of the petrol engine, and they seldom went far beyond the market town.

144 Symonds' Bus Service from Gloucester to Hucclecote and Tuffley in 1895. When this photograph was taken the horse-drawn bus had been a familiar sight on English roads for more than half a century. It was as long ago as 1829 that Shillibeer informed the chairman of the Board of Stamps: 'I am engaged in building two Vehicles after the manner of the recently established French *Omnibus*, which when completed I purpose starting on the Paddington road.' But the range of the horse-drawn bus was short. Hucclecote and Tuffley are only two or three miles from Gloucester. Nevertheless, the horse-drawn bus set its mark on the design of buses for an astonishingly long time. It is only quite recently that the motor bus has ceased to be designed to look like anything other than a horse bus with an internal-combustion engine where the horses used to be.

George Symonds, who operated these buses, was originally a publican and kept the King's Arms in Hare Lane, Gloucester, from about 1876.

145   Modern transport reaches Pulborough. This photograph is undated, but was probably taken within a year or two of Plate 146. Evidently the advantage of a motor bus as a kind of mobile billboard was less obvious in rural Sussex than it was in Lincolnshire.

146   The first motor bus to reach Caistor, Lincolnshire, in 1906. The similarity in design between this bus and its horse-drawn predecessors in Plate 144 is striking. The significant difference between the two is in their range: this bus ran from Caistor to Grimsby, a return journey of some forty miles, compared with the five or six miles return journey of Mr Symonds' horse bus.

147   The hotel bus outside the Bull's Head at Bala, Merioneth. The hotel bus survived until very recent years and probably still exists in some places. Its function was to meet guests at the railway station and bring them to the hotel. Similar vehicles could be hired in London and other big cities to call at a private house to collect a family and all its luggage and take them to a main-line terminus. One of my earliest childhood recollections is of travelling through London, on our way to a coast-bound train, in such a vehicle; the horses had been wrongly harnessed and refused to go quietly in the London traffic until we stopped and switched them round, nearside to offside. This was a great adventure for a small boy who was asked to help.

The countryman on wheels: Private transport

At first glance, horse-drawn vehicles tend to fall into two categories: those with two wheels, and those with four. In their heyday, however, they were as infinitely varied as motor cars are today and told, to the practised eye, as much as today's car does about its owner's taste, status and income. Private horse-drawn vehicles could look smart and expensive, or affluent and vulgar, or poor and hard-working, or youthful and dashing. The following pages provide a small sample of their infinite variety. Happily some of them, or vehicles like them, are still to be seen in good order at horse shows and at meets of the British Driving Society. A good example of the way in which a man's gig or other vehicle was used to place him socially is given by Thackeray in *Vanity Fair*, which was published in 1848. He is describing the transport of Major Dobbin, the reliable, persevering, but never wealthy officer who finally marries the heroine, Amelia. '"Hullo!" said he, "there's Dob's trap." The trap in question was a carriage which the Major had bought for six pounds sterling.' Even allowing for the changed value of money, this must have been the equivalent of a rather cheap secondhand car.

148   A pair of gigs at Kelvedon, Essex. The date of this photograph is uncertain, but it was probably taken about 1850 and is therefore one of the earliest photographs in the book. The photographic process required a very long exposure, during which it was inevitable that the horses should have moved their heads. The clothes tell us little of the drivers or their passenger; this was the great age of the stove-pipe hat, and it was worn by almost all sections of the community. The gigs are workman-like and in serviceable condition, and were no doubt made by a firm more accustomed to farm carts than to light carriages, but they are by no means smart, or designed to create an impression.

149　A 'two car family' of sixty years ago. Behind the farmer in this Suffolk farmyard is the equivalent in its day of the family car; evidently the farmer himself is about to use it to go out shooting. The lighter dog-cart to a donkey, on the left, scarcely has a modern equivalent. When this photograph was taken, the roads were so safe that it was normal for children much younger than these two girls to drive themselves about. Almost the only risk lay in the temperament between the shafts.

150　A ralli-car with a lady whip. Women drove then as commonly as they do now, though getting the pony harnessed was much more laborious than getting the car out of the garage. This attractive little car was about the equivalent of a Mini-Minor in its day, and just what you would have expected a countryman's wife to use for a shopping expedition or a social call.

151 A skeleton gig in Lincolnshire in about 1910. The interesting thing about this vehicle is that it is designed to carry the driver only. The use of such a vehicle was the mark of a man who wanted to cover a given distance as quickly as conditions would allow, and no nonsense; but not being able to carry a passenger would have had obvious disadvantages for such professional users as the country doctor, or for the young man with feminine company in mind.

152 A Stanhope gig of Edwardian days. Here is a good example of a vehicle designed to create a smart impression, as well as to be serviceable. It is the sort of gig that might have been used by a country doctor, though the pony has probably been bought for manners rather than for looks.

153 A governess cart in a Sussex village. Notice that the great difference between this vehicle and the five on the preceding pages is that it was entered from behind, which was easier for very young children because it avoided the moment of insecurity that was always present in mounting a gig, with its step in front of the wheel and behind the pony. According to the information that reached me with this photograph, the lady in the governess cart was in fact a governess; she does not look as though she would have stood any nonsense from her young charges.

154 Walter's motor at Mitford, Northumberland, in 1908. Walter, at the wheel, is Walter Christy, the brother-in-law of Canon MacLeod, who took the photograph and is seen in the pulpit in Plate 27. He was evidently proud, but a little self-conscious at being photographed in his new car. No doubt he maintained to his brother-in-law that these things had a future, but it is doubtful whether he can have imagined the extent of that future, or foreseen the total disruption in the pattern of English rural life, which has probably been more changed by the internal combustion engine than by any other single influence in the last five hundred years.

The countryman on wheels: Heavy duty

The heavy lorries that pound their way day and night up and down the M.1 are the descendants of a long line of transporters whose task has been, down the ages, the movement of goods through the length and breadth of England. Before them came the packhorse trains of the Middle Ages, carrying wool when wool was the lifeblood of the country's trade; the great lumbering waggons of the sixteenth and seventeenth centuries, with wheels a foot or more wide at the rim to give them a chance of traversing the thick mire of the roads; and finally, as the roads themselves grew better, the lighter, but still sturdy, vehicles that endured until the petrol engine drove them out of business. Most of them, compared with the carriages in the preceding section, remained surprisingly cumbersome and primitive.

155   Of all Victorian characters, the carrier is one of those most likely to be remembered, because it was Barkis, the carrier in Dickens's *David Copperfield*, who sent the famous message by David to Clara Peggotty: 'Barkis is willin'. Villages and remote houses that were not served by a bus were usually served by the carrier. Indeed, many houses were dependent on the carrier for supplies of household necessities, which they had sent out from the market town. This carrier, Robert Cammack, served the locality of Hatcliffe in Lincolnshire in the 1890s, when the photograph was taken.

156 Loading hops on to a waggon at Alton, Hampshire, in 1910. A reminder of how much the countryman's world depended, only half a century ago, on the muscle power of horse and man. The traditional hop-pockets are unchanged today, though they would be more likely to be loaded by a mechanical fork lift and pulled by tractor.

157 A horse-drawn fire-engine at work. This photograph was taken during a fire at a farm opposite Stibbington Hall in Huntingdonshire. The horses have been unharnessed and led away, and the engine is pumping water from the river Nene, seen in the background. The horses had had to bring this engine all the way from Stamford, a distance of about seven miles. The photograph is a reminder of why we still speak of a fire engine; in the days before piped water and fire hydrants it meant a steam pumping engine to pump water from the nearest river or pond.

158 A road hazard of a century ago. The traction-engine Hero,
described as a ten-horse-power self-propelled engine, built in 1869 by
William Tasker and Sons at Andover, Hampshire. The engine had a
chain drive, and at least two men were needed to operate it: one in
the tender and one over the front axle to steer. A third man walked
ahead with a red flag to warn of the vehicle's approach. Even a horse
accustomed to today's heavy traffic would be likely to shy on
meeting Hero. Its effects in the quiet lanes of one hundred years ago
is easy to imagine. However, the horse immediately behind in this
photograph has evidently decided that you can get used to anything.

The end of an era

159   The first men leaving Calne, Wiltshire, for the forces in August,
1914.

They sat here for a minute or two in the sunshine to have their
photograph taken; not much troubled about the future, knowing
that what they were going to do was right, and anyway that it had to
be done. We do not know how many of them — perhaps one should
say how few of them — came back. We know only too well that the
cream of their generation of countrymen died before they had had
time to reproduce themselves and to hand on their qualities to another
age. But for those who did return rural England had changed beyond
recognition, and was never to be the same again.

Index